■ DEDICATION

For Xander, fellow adventurer, road tripper, gamer, writer, and pretty much the coolest and most supportive son a mom could hope to have. I learn as much from you as I teach you. We make an amazing team, and there is no way I could imagine this without you by my side.

And for our Rawcritics community—this book would never have happened without you and your unwavering friendship and support. We are one of the most supportive and wonderful communities on the Internet. We should be so proud of that. To every single one of you, a massive Whimsey *hug* and gratitude beyond measure. Thank you!

Last but certainly not least, for my building partner, in-game tutor and protector, IRL reader and sounding board, and amazing friend, who knew about this book before I did and still managed to act surprised when I told him. jsfm, you rock, and I am more grateful than you'll ever know for all your support and encouragement.

■ ACKNOWLEDGMENTS

Many, many thanks (and buckets of love) to my son, Xander, for being so supportive and understanding and just plain awesome.

This would not have been possible without my amazing team of patient, steadfast editors. Cliff Colby, Robyn Thomas, and Scout Festa, along with all the behind-the-scenes people who have made this guide so stunning—a million thank-you's wouldn't be enough.

To my amazing family—my dad, Rolf, who never had the chance to see me published. It was his dream for me, and I know he's proud of me.

I grew up with the best of female gamer role models—my mom, June. From Munchman on one of the oldest TI computers to the newest Nintendo systems, she has never failed to inspire me (and kick my butt at games). Your support has been ever-present and ever-appreciated, and I love you.

Thanks to my awesome siblings, Didi and Terry, and my delightful nephews and niece—Chris, Ivory, Dale, and Marc—along with their families, who have shared my excitement in writing this book.

Thanks to Xander's dad, Robert Wiersema, one of my first readers, whose keen and experienced eye and unending support has been ever so appreciated. I'm so glad we can still meet across the page, be it mine or yours.

What makes me strong are my communities, and I have several—including all my friends in the Getting Higher Choir and my circle of "teacher camp" friends. You buoy me up when I'm at my lowest, and celebrate with me when I'm at my heights.

To my colleagues and families at IMHS and FFGCA—thank you. The input from families has been invaluable, and the enthusiasm and support from all those I work with immeasurable.

And finally, my Rawcritics community. Some have had a direct hand in this book—reading, editing, or contributing screenshots. And there are so many more who never fail to ask how things are going,

THE MINECRAFT GUIDE FOR PARENTS

DOWN-TO-EARTH ADVICE FOR PARENTS
OF CHILDREN PLAYING MINECRAFT

CORI DUSMANN

THE MINECRAFT GUIDE FOR PARENTS
Cori Dusmann

Peachpit Press
Find us on the web at www.peachpit.com
To report errors, please send a note to errata@peachpit.com

Peachpit Press is a division of Pearson Education.

Copyright © 2014 by Cori Dusmann

Editor: CLIFFORD COLBY
Project editor: ROBYN G. THOMAS
Copyeditor: SCOUT FESTA
Production editor: TRACEY CROOM
Compositor: MAUREEN FORYS, HAPPENSTANCE TYPE-O-RAMA
Indexer: VALERIE HAYNES PERRY
Cover design: CHARLENE CHARLES-WILL
Interior design: MAUREEN FORYS, HAPPENSTANCE TYPE-O-RAMA

ISBN-13: 978-0-321-95737-5
ISBN-10: 0-321-95737-7

9 8 7 6 5 4 3 2

Printed and bound in the United States of America

who have suggestions or have let me rant or celebrate with abandon. In particular (and no particular order, except maybe my Skype, text, and irc most recent contacts!) jsfm, creepernick, guitar, shadow, money, King, goob, MrKM, sinslave, steamboat, jhc, Axonn, Wedox, sinew, Invineron, Tyr, Rhadley, nurb, Wnhs, Anubis, Ra, Nimbalo, Neon, War, E1ectric, nelag, Tara, Jet, bionicle, jmack, CAM, Zel, zeb, Dominus, el Barto, Vernenos, Yow, SirChicken, midstorm, and everyone else I may have missed (I owe you a blog entry if I did!)— thank you, thank you, thank you! I can't wait to continue this adventure with you all.

CONTENTS

Introduction   *ix*

CHAPTER 1 ■ Let's Talk About Minecraft 1
   What Is Minecraft?   2
   Introducing Notch   3
   The Bigger Picture   5
   So Much More than a Video Game   10

CHAPTER 2 ■ The Basics of Minecraft 11
   Game Modes   12
   Multiplayer Minecraft   16
   Game Formats   17

CHAPTER 3 ■ Fitting Minecraft into Your Family 21
   My Thoughts on Technology   22
   Online Safety   32
   The Minecraft Connection   39
   Growing with Minecraft   40
   House Rules   42
   A Word on Addiction   43
   Behavior Concerns   44
   Balance   45
   Managing Rising Emotions   45
   Helping Your Child Lead the Way   55

CHAPTER 4 ■ Getting Started 57
   Things to Consider Before You Buy   58
   Purchasing Minecraft   63
   Downloading and Installing Minecraft   70

CHAPTER 5 ■ Surviving Your First Night. 73
   Game Settings   74
   Getting Started   75
   My Confession   86

CHAPTER 6 ■ Basic Gameplay **89**

Starting a New Game 90

Basic Commands 95

Biomes and Terrain 99

Mobs 104

What To Do in Minecraft 122

CHAPTER 7 ■ Digging Deeper: Technical Specifics **145**

The Minecraft Folder 146

Skins, Resource Packs, and Mods 149

CHAPTER 8 ■ Playing on Servers. **163**

Introduction to Servers 164

Home Servers 165

Minecraft Server Hosts 177

Public Servers 177

Online Safety 184

Online Communication 186

CHAPTER 9 ■ See What I Made? **195**

Sharing Online 196

CHAPTER 10 ■ The Bigger Picture **209**

Community 210

Minecraft and Education 213

Creativity 219

Video 224

MineCon and Other Gatherings 224

APPENDIX ■ Parent-Child Computer Contract **227**

Contract 228

Additions 230

Glossary *231*

Index *235*

INTRODUCTION

WELCOME TO THE WONDROUS, creative, challenging, and occasionally maddening world of Minecraft. If you are an adult who has found yourself drawn or perhaps dragged in to the world of a Minecraft-playing child or youth, you may be feeling as though you've entered a slightly askew parallel universe. Your children seem to be speaking another language, one where *biomes*, *skins*, *mods*, and *screenies* have become everyday vocabulary. Everything is now formed of pixelated cubes, from trees and livestock to the very landscape itself. And your children may alternate from being absolutely proficient at everything they do to becoming incredibly stuck, calling on you for assistance for the most confusing of activities, such as taming a cat or crafting a potion stand.

You'd like to help your child, you really would, and you know a thing or two about computers. "Check the tutorial," you might say. Or perhaps you look at the directions yourself—only to discover that this amazing game, one with literally endless possibilities and variations, does not come with a user's manual. Nor is there a tutorial, a walk-through, or any other form of guideline. It is a learn-as-you-go game, and without any idea of the purpose, the goal, or the steps to be taken, you may flounder.

In Minecraft, cats (along with dogs and many other animals) have distinct char-acteristics and uses—but taming cats is not the easiest of endeavors.

WHO IS THIS BOOK FOR?

This guide to Minecraft is designed to help parents, guardians, teach-ers, leaders, and any other adults who are being called upon to help young people in their mining and building adventures. I'll cover everything from the very basics of purchasing and installing the game to technical challenges such as updating, installing mods, and find-ing custom skins and texture packs. And I'll be sure that you actually understand what all of those things are and why they are important to the game and to your children. We'll explore the various modes of game play—Creative, Survival, and Hardcore—as well as the difficulty settings, from Peaceful to Hard (in other words, from monster free to monster intense). I'll teach you how to play the game, so you'll be able to help your child when they become stuck and you'll have the skills to log on and play alongside them should you choose to. In addition, we'll explore the less tangible side of online games like Minecraft—the questions of balance, fitting gaming into your family, navigating the world of servers and online communities, sharing work through such sites as YouTube, and much more. I'll touch on Minecraft's educational uses and explore the social side as well.

DO YOU DO WINDOWS?

When Minecraft was introduced, it was a PC game, though it was quickly expanded to run on the Mac and Linux operating systems. More recently, Minecraft Pocket Edition, for tablets and phones, was released, as was an Xbox edition. This book focuses on the original Minecraft game as designed for PC and Mac. The other versions share many components of the full game but are more limited. Directions for playing the game will be primarily Windows focused, with intructions for installation and accessing files on Macs as well.

WHO AM I?

I wear many hats—in a large nutshell, I'm a childcare provider, a child and youth counselor, a writer, a gamer, and a homeschooling mom. Whenever I can combine any of those passions, I'm as happy as can be, and I'm fortunate enough to be able to do so much of the time.

Under the username Whimseysgirl, I play Minecraft both on my own and with my son, Xander (who goes by Wrednax). We are part of an amazing community on Rawcritics, a family-friendly server (primarily for players age 11 and older), though we also play single-player games and venture onto other servers. Minecraft has been something we've shared from the beginning, and it has become a source of common ground with the kids I work with as well.

■ HOW I BECAME INVOLVED IN MINECRAFT

When Xander was 11 (as I write this he's 14), he was already pretty computer savvy. I've been a haphazard but avid gamer since childhood (though less seriously in recent years), so he's grown up in a house where gaming is just part of the culture. Since I teach him at home, the computer is an important learning tool as well as a toy, and he was well able to navigate it from early on, often faster than I could.

Xander was and is very interested in gaming, vlogs, blogs, and popular-culture websites and seems to always have a finger on the pulse of the gaming community. He knows how to do his research, and he knows the value of checking reviews or opinion pieces and of seeking more than one answer to a question.

When Xander started showing me pictures and videos of this new game he was interested in, Minecraft, I was less than impressed. It was still in its earliest version. The company was hoping to raise money to expand the game and release a beta version. Their marketing seemed basic, and when I watched video clips or saw pictures, those pixelated cubes seemed positively simplistic and outdated. But Xander continued to explore it, and soon enough the story of this new game, with its small independent game designer taking a chance, had me in its thrall too. We ordered a copy.

Suddenly we found ourselves well into the unknown—not only were there no directions, but even fan-made YouTube tutorials were scarce at that point. The learning curve was steep. But Xander soon learned the ropes and began playing in earnest, creating cool structures and farming, mining, and exploring. I started my own game, slowly learning as I went and often calling on his expertise.

In Minecraft, large cubes are the basis of everything. Decorating a tree means giving up the notion of rounded ornaments.

It wasn't until Xander discovered online servers, though, that I became truly involved in his gaming. Until then he'd played only on his own. The idea that he was playing with strangers and conversing with them in game chats was worrying to me. Although I'm far from being a controlling parent, I do like to know who he's playing with and what he's doing. He settled on the Rawcritics.com server, a family-friendly community that offers a PVP (player versus player) world as well as a more peaceful build world. And I was right there watching over his shoulder to see what he'd gotten himself into.

What he found astounded me. It was a community, a true community, with players of all ages. There were staff keeping an eye on things and providing support and activities. There were groups, factions, and teams gathering and pooling resources, creating amazing builds, and banding together in battles and raids to protect their creations and materials. Yes, there was drama and some negative attitudes between players, but there was also caring, friendship, and mutual support. Players knew that I was watching and commenting over Xander's shoulder, and they began to ask if they could show me their work and their skins (the appearance of their characters in the game), drawing me in to their community alongside Xander. I watched him slowly gain confidence and ambition until he started his own town—a town that grew and gained members under his leadership.

It was then that I realized the potential of Minecraft to be far more than a simple building game. It could be an educational tool, a creative outlet, a social platform, and so much more. There was space to work independently as well as with others. By that point there were countless communities and servers, and people were making YouTube tutorials and game walk-throughs, and even writing songs and making music videos. Inspiration, passion, and creativity were abounding, and it really had me thinking about the ever-changing role of technology and gaming in our lives. It also had me thinking about Internet safety, about communication between Xander and me, and about my role as an educator and the parent of a pre-teen in this new age of digitally connected peers.

■ MY MOTIVATION IN WRITING THIS BOOK

In addition to homeschooling Xander, I've worked with kids and teens for over 20 years in a variety of settings, from daycares to classrooms to a psychiatric hospital. My roles have ranged from care worker to educational assistant to school-age daycare manager. I've watched children and families get swept into gaming and the online world, and I've seen it become both a source of battles and a place of learning and connection. I've seen parents and children become hooked on online activities, and I am aware of the need for balance, but I've also seen people gain confidence through their experiences in online communities. Navigating the positives and negatives, finding balance, creating dialogue and communication—those are of vital importance too.

Xander eventually convinced me to get my own Minecraft account. I joined his server, and immediately we were playing, working, and creating together. I soon formed friendships with players on the server—some were Xander's friends and others were strictly my own. It was exciting to be able to work and play with him, but at the same time it was exceedingly frustrating.

Watching over his shoulder had given me much of the knowledge I needed, but I soon discovered I didn't have the skills. I was slow and clumsy. I died—a lot. I got lost in caves and on land. I struggled with updates and maps. I was constantly referring to video tutorials, wiki pages, and fellow players, many of whom are much closer to Xander's age and far more computer savvy than I can ever hope to be. I once again saw the need for a guide, something that I could refer to when I got stuck.

Whimseysgirl and Wrednax

Since then, I've become more competent but certainly not proficient. My lack of skills is a bit of a running joke on our server, but I manage to stay alive, create bigger and better builds, and support new players who need help. Xander and I play together and apart, but we constantly share what we're working on. A wonderful and unexpected bonus is being able to connect in a completely different way with the children in the afterschool program where I work. Our discussions about Minecraft give us a positive common ground—once they finish grilling me to ensure that I am genuine and not a gaming poser. In addition, I've been able to help their parents navigate this confusing new world, assuaging their concerns and helping them support their children.

I'm looking forward to doing the same for you. I hope to help you find ways to connect with your child through this amazing game, even if you never mine or place a single block yourself—though I certainly encourage you to give it a try; you might be pleasantly surprised!

LET'S TALK ABOUT MINECRAFT

OVER THE PAST THREE YEARS, a small independent video game has managed to gain as much attention as so-called "A-list" games released by some of the largest developers and companies in the world. With over 20 million copies sold and thousands more being bought every day, Minecraft has defied the pundits and become one of the most successful pieces of entertainment software ever created. But what exactly is this game that has captured the interest of players young and old?

WHAT IS MINECRAFT?

Minecraft is what is known as a *sandbox* game—that is, it takes place in an open world where the player has complete freedom to explore and create and isn't restricted to an existing storyline. In Minecraft, players acquire resources, build, explore, and create anything they wish (within the parameters of the game, of course). There is no plot or storyline, and there are no set goals or activities that must be completed (although those that play Minecraft have found myriad ways of creating goals and activities). In short, Minecraft is a completely open environment in which to create and play while constantly interacting with other human players from all over the world.

When players log in, they find themselves in a world formed of one-meter cubes (**Figure 1.1**), which are known in the game as *blocks*. These blocks are made from a variety of materials—from dirt, sand, and stone found underfoot to the trees and plants scattered across the landscape. The world is randomly generated, so it is never the same, and it features a variety of biomes, including snowy, desert, and forest. Also scattered across the land are animals such as cows, sheep, and chickens. And at night, if the game isn't set to Peaceful, the monsters (or, as they're known in Minecraft, *mobs*) come out. Zombies, skeletons, giant spiders, and the green, exploding creepers add a level of difficulty to staying alive as you traverse the Minecraft landscape. From building a shelter to finding resources, there are many basic tasks to tackle as soon as the game begins—and that's just the beginning of what Minecraft has to offer.

FIGURE 1.1 A one-meter cube, the building block of Minecraft

Minecraft is written in the relatively accessible programming language Java. This means that anyone with basic programming knowledge can write modifications, or *mods*, for the game that can range anywhere from small changes that don't affect gameplay to massive alterations and additions that shift the entire nature of the gaming experience. Minecraft players have embraced the opportunities that such coding provides, and there are now thousands of mods that can be downloaded.

This combination of freedom in the very core of gameplay and the addition of endless options in mods means that Minecraft can be whatever the gamer desires. Add to that the special adventure maps that are available and the countless *servers*—websites that allow gamers to play together and which turn single-player games into multiplayer ones (more on these later)—and there truly is something for every player.

So where did such a creative, open game originate? In a time when the big game developers embrace elaborate plots and structured games, how did this little independent game rise to such heights? Read on, intrepid Minecraft aficionado!

INTRODUCING NOTCH

In May 2009, Swedish independent game developer Markus Persson released a demonstration version of Minecraft. It was a very basic game at that point, though all the main creative features were already taking form. He began to sell the still-in-development game at the low cost of 10 British pounds (about $15 USD) to raise funds to further develop it. Those buyers were assured free upgrades for life.

Game sales took off, and soon Persson was able to leave his job and work full time on developing Minecraft, hiring other game developers and releasing two other versions before the far more complete

Alpha edition was released in June, 2010. Sales of the early versions reached 200,000 copies, an almost unheard-of amount for an independent game still in development. Persson, along with Carl Manneh and Jakob Porser, launched the video-game company Mojang that summer, and in December 2010 they released the Beta version of Minecraft.

When Minecraft was officially released in November 2011, it had sold over one and a half million copies. Not too shabby for a small independent game. Persson, who is known in Minecraft circles as Notch (**Figure 1.2**), has since passed the Minecraft torch to a new team of developers, led by Jens Bergensten. The game is constantly being upgraded, with additions and changes occurring with every update.

FIGURE 1.2 Minecraft 1.0.0, with its signature ever-changing yellow comment—in this case proclaiming its creation by Notch

Fast-forward to 2013, and Minecraft has sold over 20 million copies and shows no signs of slowing down. No wonder that Persson and Bergensten ended up on the 2013 "*Time* 100," *Time* magazine's annual list of the 100 most influential people in the world. Persson continues to work on games, and he promotes independent game developers, speaking up against the large companies in defense of the independents. He has proven himself to be an inspiration and role model for up-and-coming developers, and he has started many a young person on the path of programming and game development.

THE BIGGER PICTURE

So now we've looked at the very basics of what Minecraft is and how it came to be. But that is just the tip of the iceberg. Yes, Minecraft is simply a video game, and at first glance a very basic game at that. But it is what can be done with it that truly astounds, and begins to explain its popularity.

■ IT'S A WHOLE NEW WORLD

Players can work independently on whatever they choose, but with the availabilty of servers (multiplayer online Minecraft worlds), they can also join up with others who share a similar vision. The collaborative server of WesterosCraft, for example, has become a gathering place for fans of the *Game of Thrones* television series (**Figure 1.3**). Players have created a scale model of the world featured in George R. R. Martin's *A Song of Ice and Fire* books and the incredibly popular television series that is based on them. The model stretches the equivalent of 500 miles, with buildings created in exquisite detail. Other servers host battle-like competitions based on themes such as the *Hunger Games* books and movies and the Team Fortress video games. These servers have played an important role in connecting solitary Minecraft players, changing the face of the game. ·

FIGURE 1.3 A small portion of the community-built WesterosCraft world

What Minecraft offers—and what most video games fundamentally cannot—is a way for players to create. And not just create using small, restricted methods, such as being able to select the details of your character's appearance from a menu; Minecraft offers complete artistic freedom to design entire worlds in any manner you choose. Players can be artists, architects, engineers, designers, and so much more. In fact the scope and depth of Minecraft continue to evolve, with new (and ususally clever) concepts introduced with reliable regularity.

Most players start independently, playing in a single-player world and learning how to mine for materials and work with blocks. Builds (locations created by a player) start small and simple, and then become more and more elaborate as the player develops skills. With fancier builds comes a player's need to share what they've been working on. The desire to share work, or perhaps to work with others, often leads players to seek out multiplayer servers or to post their work in blogs or on YouTube.

Wrednax

I'VE BEEN BUILDING for about two years now. My most recent build, which I've spent about three months on, is the Tower of Babel from the 1927 German silent film *Metropolis*. It's given me a really cool chance to play with the Art Deco architecture style (**Figure 1.4**), and it's also shown me how much can be done with different styles in Minecraft.

FIGURE 1.3 Wrednax's Tower of Babel

■ COMMUNITY

Something that has arisen, not just through Minecraft but across the Internet, is a sense of community that has nothing to do with physical proximity. Minecraft has spawned a plethora of such connections and communities. Through online tutorials and wiki pages, multiplayer servers that can host hundreds of people, and chat rooms and forums, Minecraft players are connecting, talking, and playing together.

YOUTUBE AND LIVESTREAMING

Since early on in the development of Minecraft, people have explored the many ways they could use YouTube. Some gamers record themselves playing Minecraft. Others make tutorials, videos with step-by-step directions for everything from installing games to crafting tools or making elaborate builds. And still others use YouTube to share songs or parodies they've created; there are now well over a hundred songs about either Minecraft itself or jingles that tell stories from a fictional Minecraft character's point of view.

In addition, there are now livestream websites, where players share their games—live—with online viewers. Viewers log in to a streaming website, and the player's game is visible in a window on the stream page, sometimes with a smaller window that shows the player as well. There is usually a chat window on the screen, which allows viewers to interact with each other and leave comments for the player. Streams are often recorded and posted on YouTube.

MULTIPLAYER SERVERS AND ONLINE FORUMS

There are other ways that players connect with one another. Multiplayer servers such as Rawcritics (the one Wrednax and I play on) abound. Simple Minecraft servers are not very challenging to set up, and players can be limited to an invitation-only list. Parents can and do set up servers that are only for members of their family or for their children and children's friends. At the other end of the spectrum are multiplayer servers that host hundreds or thousands of gamers. Gamers communicate with one another using onscreen chat.

Many servers also have forums where people can share ideas, hold longer conversations, and discuss anything under the sun. For example, the Rawcritics forums (**Figure 1.5**) are very eclectic, with topics ranging from server brainstorming and problem-solving to detailed conversations about other games to incredibly elaborate lore about the player-versus-player world (one of several types of Minecraft worlds on Rawcritics). Indeed, there are even discussions about epic videos, and for those who want to take a stroll into left field, a thread dedicated to all things *My Little Pony*.

FIGURE 1.5 The Rawcritics.com home page

MORE MINECRAFT ONLINE

Minecraft *wikis*—websites that allow their content to be added to and modified—attempt to answer questions related to the game. These can be great resources, and we'll look at them in more detail later. There are also how-to guides and all manner of user-made sites. Minecraft players can connect easily with each other and find players with similar interests. And many of these servers, websites, and forums are family friendly, creating safe places for younger players to start interacting with the larger Internet community.

Another amazing aspect of Minecraft is its use in the classroom. Teachers are developing curricula that use Minecraft not just to teach computer skills, but to teach social skills, demonstrate cell structures, and show historical timelines. Even to those of us highly engaged in cutting–edge education, Minecraft continues to impress and amaze.

SO MUCH MORE THAN A VIDEO GAME

It's clear that Minecraft has had a dramatic and sweeping effect in a very short time. People are using this unique piece of software to design and build all manner of structures, from soaring castles to in-game music boxes and even functional in-game 8-bit computers. Even those who would say they don't have a creative bone in their body are finding themselves inspired. And perhaps more importantly, players are connecting with each other and are sharing their work and their ideas in ways that were previously unheard of. And I haven't even mentioned the people behind the scenes who write code—creating mods, additional game content, and texture packs that change the appearance of the game—or the ones who design, host, and staff the servers, often volunteering their time and energy to ensure that players have safe and stable game environments. The Minecraft community is a strong one and has added much to the game itself, and the community and the developers are engaged in a sort of organic symbiosis where they are driving each other to create a product/tool/game that is unique to the world.

CHAPTER 2

THE BASICS OF MINECRAFT

A BIG PART of what makes Minecraft so irresistible is the large number of gameplay options available to the player. From a peaceful and creative experience in which nothing needs to be done but build, to a hardcore survival mode in which players must mine and craft all the materials and tools they need (and everything in between), there is something for everyone.

GAME MODES

When starting a single-player game of Minecraft, you need to create a new world. You are given the option to name your world and select which game mode you would like to play in—Creative, Survival, or Hardcore. It is possible to switch your world from one mode to another mid-game, so you're not locked in to one type of play after you make your initial selection.

■ CREATIVE

When playing in Creative mode, you have open access to endless supplies of every type of building material in the game. You can terra-form, clear land, add mountains, or fill in lakes—all block by block. You could build that dream house you've always imagined or create a mighty dungeon in the Nether (the lava-filled underworld of Minecraft) (**Figure 2.1**).

FIGURE 2.1 The Nether

In Creative mode, you don't have to worry about facing monsters, starving to death, or any of the other hazards that you encounter when playing in Survival mode. Mobs, including all the monsters, do spawn (pop into existence out of nowhere) in Creative mode, but they can't harm you. You don't need to mine for resources, nor do you need to grow and eat food. Everything is provided through a comprehensive menu, allowing players to simply focus on constructing and creating. Another feature found only in Creative mode is flight. Flying allows for much easier building, because you can work on tall builds without the need to create stairs or ladders, and without fear of falling. You can build structures in the sky or towering spires with ease.

Creative mode is perfect for younger players or for those not interested in the survival aspects of the game. Creating large, resource-heavy builds is easier because you do not have to acquire all the materials. Creative mode is also a great place to experiment with ideas, such as making a rough draft of a build before constructing it on a survival map. It's also a good place to play with *redstone*, a resource that allows players to create basic and complex circuitry. The options are virtually endless in Creative mode.

■ SURVIVAL

Survival mode has a very different focus when compared to Creative mode. When playing in Survival mode, you can still build whatever you'd like, but you'll need to find, mine, or craft the resources and tools first. Players gather materials for their inventory and create chests to store items. You can craft many items, using tools such as a crafting bench, furnace, or potion stand while following guidelines known as *recipes*. For example, to make iron tools or armor, you need to get wood from a tree (by hitting it with your bare fists); make a crafting bench; make a wooden pickaxe; mine for stone, coal, and iron ore; craft a furnace; and smelt your iron ore using the coal you found. Only

then can you craft iron items (**Figure 2.2**). It sounds far more complicated than it is, but for new players, such a sequence of steps can feel
overwhelming.

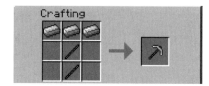

FIGURE 2.2 Crafting iron tools

Survival mode is the only mode in which you can change your
difficulty level, choosing one of four levels: Peaceful, Easy, Normal,
or Hard. Depending on your difficulty setting, at night you may need
to either hide from or fight mobs of zombies or skeletons. And you
need to make sure that you have food so you don't starve. Shelter and
food are two priorities in Survival mode, so some form of a farm will
likely be one of your first projects. If you're not playing on the Peaceful
setting, armor and weapons will also be important.

When you die in Survival mode, you *respawn* (start over) at your
spawn point (the point at which you started the game). Any items you
were carrying when you died will remain at your point of death for a
while, so you might be able to reclaim them—unless you died in lava,
in which case they probably burned. This is one of the more frustrating
aspects of Survival mode, and players quickly learn not to carry all their
valuables with them. It is also possible to create a new spawn point
(where you will return upon dying) by crafting a bed and sleeping in it.

SURVIVAL DIFFICULTY SETTINGS

In Survival mode, there are different levels of difficulty, which are accessed through the Options menu. We'll revisit this topic in Chapter 4, but a quick overview will give you a sense of the choices available.

Note that in Survival mode, players have a health meter, which indicates how healthy they are (measured in heart icons), and a food bar, which indicates how hungry they are. The difficulty settings affect how these bars work, and the bar levels affect how much damage the mobs inflict when they attack.

Peaceful. The name of this setting says it all. On the Peaceful setting, there are no hostile mobs. This means that monsters will not spawn within the game, though there are still peaceful mobs, such as chickens and cows. Although players can die by falling, drowning, or being stuck in lava, they can't be killed by roving spiders or skeletons. Players don't get hungry or risk dying of starvation. They can take damage, such as from falls, but their health regenerates. This is a good setting for younger players who want to experience the mining and crafting aspects of the game. Parents who don't want any hint of violence should note that players kill the animals to attain such materials as pork and leather.

Easy. When you're playing on the Easy setting, hostile mobs spawn and cause damage to players, though it's not very severe. If the hunger bar empties, the player's heart meter will drop to five hearts (from ten).

Normal is the baseline setting. Mobs cause a fair bit of damage, but it's damage that players can recover from—unless there is a cumulative effect and they don't have time to heal. Hearts on the health meter will regenerate when the hunger bar is full; when the hunger bar is empty, players will lose hearts until they have only half of their hearts left.

Hard. On the Hard setting, the mobs are much more powerful and cause greater damage. Players can die of starvation if they let their health meter become empty.

■ HARDCORE

The final game mode in Minecraft is Hardcore. Hardcore is exactly as it sounds; it is the extreme version of Minecraft. The difficulty setting is the same as the Hard setting in Survival mode, so the gameplay itself isn't harder than that setting. However, unlike Survival mode, where you respawn at death, when a player dies in Hardcore, the game is over. The world is closed, and any builds or items are lost. Some third-party programs allow you to access your build if the loss is monumental, but Hardcore isn't the best mode for designing epic structures; those are better done in Creative or Survival mode. Hardcore is about surviving in the most challenging of Minecraft circumstances—well, the most challenging circumstances that can be found on a regular single-player game, at least.

MULTIPLAYER MINECRAFT

Although there are many options for gameplay within Minecraft itself, it isn't until you explore the multiplayer option that the full scale and scope of the game becomes clear.

Players can create their own servers or join existing ones. When playing on a server, players interact with each other using an in-game chat. Some servers are collaborative build servers, whereas others are fighting servers, such as player-versus-player worlds. There are servers based on themes that range from *My Little Pony* to *Star Trek*. Some servers are communities of thousands of people, and others work on a much smaller scale, as in a family server set up for a single group of friends.

Servers can be completely open, or closed except to certain players. Often they are moderated and staffed by players who use special commands to keep order and offer help when needed. Navigating the world of servers can be a tricky one for parents and kids, but there are plenty of well-moderated, family-friendly servers (such as the server Wrednax and I play on). We'll explore how to find them in Chapter 7.

There is another flavor of servers called LAN servers. LAN stands for Local Area Network and is a local group of computers connected over a network. "Local" in this context means in the same room or in the same house; "connected" means short-range Wi-Fi network or Cat 5 cabling (Ethernet cables). LAN servers can be a real hoot and are actually a lot of fun, especially if you have a bunch of friends who are all willing to come to your place and bring their computers so you can connect and play Minecraft together.

GAME FORMATS

Minecraft has expanded far beyond its original, Windows-based state. From apps for phones and tablets to an edition for the Xbox 360, players now have many ways to craft and play.

■ WINDOWS AND MAC

When Minecraft was first released, it was designed for the Windows operating system. Mac and Linux versions soon followed. These versions of Minecraft need to be purchased through the Mojang website, but gift cards are now available at some stores, so buyers don't need a credit card to buy an account. Buying the game requires that the purchaser set up a user account and a user name that will identify them when playing the game (for example, Whimseysgirl for myself and Wrednax for my son). Each purchase is for one user account.

The concept of one account/one player can be confusing to new players and can often cause frustration for families in which there are a couple of people using one account. Firstly, only one person can play at a time. And more importantly, if clear boundaries are not established, players sharing an account can destroy each other's work or otherwise wreak havoc in the game. For this reason, it might be reasonable to consider purchasing more than one account if multiple children want to play or if a parent and child are interested in playing together. Accounts make good gifts, or could be something children can save toward.

MINECRAFT POCKET EDITION

Minecraft Pocket Edition (**Figure 2.3**) is the mobile app for phones and tablets. Much cheaper than purchasing an account, this is often the version parents buy first. Although it shares many features found in the full game, it is not the same game by any means. Some aspects of Minecraft are completely omitted, such as redstone circuits, and some block types are not available. The game is played using the touchscreen, but basic gameplay, such as placing and removing blocks, hasn't changed. This is a great way to introduce kids to Minecraft and to get them building and creating, although chances are high that they'll ask for the full game at some point (which is certainly not a bad thing).

FIGURE 2.3 Minecraft Pocket Edition

RASPBERRY PI MINECRAFT At the time of this writing, there is a Raspberry Pi version of Minecraft in the works that's based on the Pocket Edition of Minecraft. This version allows players to play on a Raspberry Pi (an indie micro computer that is priced under $50 and can give new programmers an easy and flexible platform to create on), but it also allows the Raspberry Pi to be used as a Minecraft server. Exciting stuff!

■ XBOX 360 EDITION

Minecraft Xbox 360 Edition is the only console version of Minecraft. While most basic gameplay features are the same, some differences stand out. The worlds are limited in size, and the method of crafting items is different. Unlike any of the other versions, Minecraft Xbox 360 Edition has a tutorial. It also has a split-screen function that allows for multiple players.

One large component of Minecraft that the Pocket and Xbox 360 editions lack is the ability for mods to be written for the game. All the extra content—the servers, the special games, the texture packs, and the various mods—is available only within the full game.

■ SONY PS3/PS4 EDITION

At the time of this writing, Sony announced that Minecraft is indeed headed to the Sony PlayStation 4 console as well as the PS3 and Vita platforms. The only caveat to this is that Sony has not set a specific date, but by the time you are reading this it may be available on these Sony platforms.

CHAPTER **3**

FITTING MINECRAFT INTO YOUR FAMILY

LIFE IS BUSY for families these days. Between work, school, daycare, homework, extracurricular activities, chores, and family time, sometimes it's a surprise that we find time to sleep at all. And screen time has always had a bad reputation, so it's no wonder that it ends up at the bottom of the list.

Like other computer entertainment products, Minecraft can be very addictive for kids (and adults!), so care must be taken to ensure that it does not consume your children's lives. That being said, it has much to offer in terms of creativity, goal setting, building and design, spatial awareness, and—if kids are playing on a server— social interaction and community building. Even if your kids never get on an "outside" Minecraft server, the game has a tendency to drive a great deal of interaction and discussion among those in the room while the game's being played. Indeed, creative, interactive, and even heated discussions about the best way to solve an in-game problem are more the norm than the exception in many households. These exchanges make it difficult for anyone to argue that there isn't a social element to Minecraft. Kids and adults can learn a lot about working together and group problem-solving by tackling some Minecraft challenges together.

Finding ways to fit Minecraft into your family's lives in ways that meet everyone's wants and needs can be a challenge, but it is possible. Technology has become an integral part of our lives, making it even more important that we thoughtfully—rather than resentfully— create space for it.

I'll get to Minecraft, balance, online safety, and house rules in a bit, but I have some broader thoughts I'd like to share first.

MY THOUGHTS ON TECHNOLOGY

My views on video games and screen time in general don't follow the party line that kids are spending too much time in front of screens, that they're losing touch with others, and that screen time is detrimental and must be carefully guarded. To me, there is a vast difference between being mindlessly entertained by something on a television screen and being actively engaged and interacting with media.

I believe that balance is important and that we need to leave space for physical activities and creative play. But there is much value to be found in technology, from both educational and social perspectives.

THE CHANGING ROLE OF TECHNOLOGY

Technology has changed greatly over the past few decades, and it is very different from the technology that today's parents grew up with. In much of the world, technology is pervasive and intertwined with our day-to-day activities. We all use screens: phones are much more than basic communication devices; tablets and laptops have become an integral part of many jobs; we turn to technology to shop, order groceries or meals, check bus schedules, organize our days, plan our recreation, and learn. And not surprisingly we turn to technology for our entertainment: we watch programs and play games, use social media, and share our lives with friends, family, and sometimes the world. Children watch their parents using technology all the time— and then become frustrated when their screen time is curtailed by parents who seemingly have no sense of the importance of technology in their children's lives.

The reality is that while adults are using technology to make their days a little smoother, youth are using technology with greater speed, ease, and control than the adults around them. They have higher expectations of what technology can do for them, and they often have better skills at accessing it. While they may enjoy some television shows or movies, kids for the most part aren't content to sit in front of a TV and be entertained anymore. Now they want to interact with the programs directly, both responding to and receiving feedback. But there are drawbacks—some children (and adults) now find it a struggle to do things without that immediate feedback. This is where balance is important, and acknowledging the positive aspects of technology is important too.

Wrednax

I HAVE DYSLEXIA, a condition which makes reading and writing more difficult. Playing retro games like Pokémon on my Nintendo DS was what got me reading for myself, because the game was a lot easier and more fun once I was able to read the plot.

From there, I started reading through novels at a high pace, and now I can read an adult novel in a day. If it weren't for video games, I'm not sure how long it would have taken me to learn to read.

■ DEGREES OF SCREEN TIME

We've long been aware that spending too much time in front of screens should be discouraged. We need to monitor how much time our children spend in front of a screen, but much more importantly, we need to pay attention to what our children are doing, what they're watching or playing, and how they're using that screen time.

Television and movies are passive entertainment. We may be learning from what we watch—depending on the topic, the material, and the manner in which it is imparted—but it is completely passive. To make it less so, we need to discuss the program, research further, or find other ways to interact with the information. It's great to watch a show about a far-off land and culture, but unless we talk about it or do some further exploring in books or online, chances are that we'll forget most of what we saw. And if we're tired or just looking for a way to relax, chances are high we'll select shows that are pure entertainment.

The same is true for children. Set them in front of the television and turn it on; more often than not, a familiar expression crosses their faces: eyes glaze, mouths relax and drop open, bodies slump. Getting their attention is a challenge, and they seem not to hear their names being called. And this applies to adults too, although we might not want to acknowledge that fact. The exception, usually only for smaller children, is when the programming is interactive, such as when characters onscreen ask questions or invite the children to dance or sing or join in other activities. Game shows sometimes have a similar effect on adults, who might try to answer questions before the contestants do. But in most cases, when we sit in front of the television we too display those glazed eyes, slack jaws, and slumped bodies.

In contrast, watch children playing a computer or video game. Their bodies are more alert; they lean forward and constantly move in little ways. Their eyes are active. A tongue may stick out in concentration. They respond to what is happening on the screen in dynamic ways, rather than being passive. This can still be relaxing, however, despite being interactive and active. It all depends on the activity.

At times we may become too obsessed with what is happening on our screens, when we find ourselves a little too engaged and things make us frustrated or even angry. When we lose something we've invested time and energy in, or when we get stuck and can't progress, we find ourselves reacting emotionally. This is something we need to pay special attention to, to make sure that we keep screen time in perspective.

I enjoy my time in front of screens, whether it be watching a favorite program, using social media to connect with friends, or playing a game. It is important to Xander as well. I have a habit of allowing screen time to take over physical recreation, and I need to make an effort to get us off the screens and moving at times. I would much prefer Xander be less passively entertained and more interactive. But when it comes to screen time, I encourage computer use over television. And yes, some of that time is spent passively watching YouTube videos, but for the most part those too are much more interactive. His preference is to watch vloggers (video bloggers) doing walkthroughs of games he plays or has an interest in. More often than not, he has a vlog or game walkthrough running on one monitor while he's doing something on the other monitor.

I can hear some of you wonder at that—information and screen overload! I felt the same until I paid attention and realized that for Xander, this is an optimum learning environment. His brain is busy and moves fast, and when he is learning something or really needs to focus, he finds it much easier to do so when the busy part of his brain is somewhat occupied with music, videos, or something a little passive. When I first started to pay attention to this, I noticed how much more he can focus with something going on in the background. The same is true for him when he's not on the computer. Looking back I know that this has always been the case. I have no idea if this is the way he's wired or if I inadvertently helped create the neural pathways he has.

While Xander thrives on background sounds and is an auditory learner, I am the complete opposite. I rarely even think to put on music, let alone seek out background noise. I can tune out sounds with great ease, but I'm very much a visual learner—that same skill of ignoring noise can be a detriment when I inadvertently tune out auditory information. Being aware of your children's and your own learning style can make a world of difference, because you can help them create the best learning and working environment for their needs.

When Xander was little, his activity of choice was Lego. He could spend hours building and creating. It was pointless to buy him other toys, because they'd sit unused. Xander also always loved, and still does, being read aloud to. By the time he was in kindergarten we were well into chapter books, and he wanted stories all the time. There was only so much reading aloud I could do, so I started looking for audiobooks.

I wonder whether the need to have other things occupying part of his brain was nature or nurture. He burned through shorter books like *Charlie and the Chocolate Factory* and anything else by Roald Dahl. I'm a fantasy fan, so we moved on to C.S. Lewis's Narnia books, then on to the Harry Potter series. I'm aware that these children's books are very mature for a 5- or 6-year-old, but I believe that imagery in stories is far less damaging than imagery onscreen. Although he was listening to Harry Potter face Voldemort at the age of 5, he wasn't allowed to watch any onscreen violence, not even the *Star Wars* movies or other shows that children watch at a young age now. If you listen to a narrative description of a fight but have never seen one, it is pretty difficult to imagine any details, as you have absolutely no point of reference.

Xander, while building and creating with Lego, managed to listen to hundreds of novels as he was growing up. And during the day in his free time, he always elected to have stories in the background rather than music. One of the first things he learned to do on the computer was play audiobooks. Although I was skeptical at first, he was paying attention—the discussions we had about the books were detailed and thoughtful. His vocabulary grew daily, as did his somewhat British accent, as most of the books were read by British actors.

And so the seeds were planted, or the discovery was made, that led to Xander learning much more easily when running something in the background. And today, as often as not it's still an audiobook he has going. That learning style fits his needs, and I respect that he knows what works best for him, particularly because I have observed how successful he is in his optimal learning environment and how much he struggles when he is not. Helping your children understand their needs in a learning environment gives them a valuable tool that they will be able to use all their lives.

Not all screen time is the same. Interactive time can be far more productive than passive, and there can and should be space for that in our days, particularly if you have a tendency to default to television time while dinner is being made, or as a reward. You may find that they, and you, are much happier playing something interactive rather than just passively watching.

PLAY IS CHILDREN'S WORK

The idea that play is children's work is a deeply rooted belief for many educators, particularly those working with younger children. It is a system of thinking that is being discarded by education systems in favor of more formal academic programming. Where kindergarten classrooms were once filled with shelves of creative toys, such as blocks and dolls, and kids came home with artistic projects almost daily, we now find stations, each one designed with a specific learning outcome in mind and a specific task that must be accomplished.

I have to wonder if a learning station designed to encourage collaboration through a group project is any more effective than children being given free rein with a pile of cardboard boxes and rolls of tape, or children playing a game of make-believe in a play kitchen.

I am not suggesting that the academic route is lesser, but I do feel that we are moving too far toward rote learning and removing creativity and expression from education. Balance is vital, and I fear that the scale is tipping too far in one direction. It has long been known that children learn from being able to interact with their environment, explore, and make discoveries. We all learn best when we are actively engaged in an activity we are keenly interested in. Spend even an hour in a play-based children's program (these usually end by kindergarten, unfortunately), and you will see endless examples of children actively and creatively learning as they play, with joyful abandon and endless curiosity and no idea that they are learning as they play.

What we see as perhaps a waste of valuable time is vitally important to children. We fill their days with activities, and we spend our time worrying that they don't have the same skills as their peers—that by choosing one class we might be keeping them from learning something else. There can be balance between classes and time to play. And play, for children, is also work.

Technology is now part of children's play. I don't just mean games in particular, but rather exploring and discovering what technology has to offer, learning how to navigate a computer (and from there the Internet), playing independently and with others, and learning different ways to communicate, collaborate, and solve problems. These are skills that can't be formally taught as easily as they can be learned through play. They are learned through experience: on the playground, in the home, going through daily activities, and, yes, through technology as well.

▦ WHAT'S REALLY GOING ON ONLINE?

There comes a time when kids surpass their parents in navigating the Internet to find, process, and share information. It seems to happen around 11 years old, give or take a year. At about this point, parents who are taken by surprise at the skills their kids have often try to rein them in by controlling their screen time or setting stronger limits—or they stop trying to control them at all. Somewhere in the middle lies a balance that needs to be reached, because the Internet is an amazing and powerful tool in the hands of our youth, but one that requires supervision and discussion.

Beyond simply being entertained by online games and videos, children and teens are discovering how to write basic programs, write mods for games, and create complete games. They are making and editing videos and posting them on YouTube. They are connecting and communicating with others all around the world— people of all ages, races, gender, social and financial standing—and other barriers don't matter. There are amazing things happening online every minute of the day, and kids and teens are at the center of much of it. They're being creative through games, art, music, drama, and writing. They're taking political stands and asking difficult questions. They're experimenting and pushing the bounds of science. And the crazy thing is, so many of their parents and teachers have no idea this is happening.

I talk to teens every day. In Minecraft I watch them create cities and nations on servers. I watch them work together to build amazing creations and to make videos of games they're playing. I see them support each other and, yes, sometimes tear each other down (though that happens less often). I see the hours they put in: hosting a server, maintaining an online presence to help other players, streaming live video, being responsible for all the viewers who come along, building new maps and games, working together in games to gather resources, and buying and selling goods to foster a lively economy. They have responsibilities and duties. They have people who count on them. They must prove themselves good leaders. They must work together. These things fill me with pride, and I'm not even a parent to these kids. And beyond all that, there is a worldwide community that is growing larger every day.

Wrednax

ON THE RAWCRITICS player-versus-player (PVP) world, I based a town on the design of the Tower of Babel from the 1927 silent film *Metropolis* (I love the Art Deco architecture of the movie). My town was built above the remains of a previous town buried deep underground. Alas, after many weeks of work on the tower, I never managed to finish it, and now the server is updating the map, so I'll be starting from scratch.

I wanted my town to be part of a nation that wasn't led by a single person, but rather by a council of people. I was given my nation by another player who was quitting the server. I sent messages to several other towns on the subject of joining an *oligarchical* nation (a nation or country led by a small group of people); most of them agreed to join. I wrote a constitution soon after everyone joined so we would have a firm basis for law. Our server will be starting a new PVP map, and I am already recruiting different members to a new town and nation.

We hear about cyber-bullying, and it is a very real, very serious problem that is part of the darker side of technology. We also fear cyber predators, and they too exist. There are things we need to be watchful for. But what we don't hear about are the online communities of kids, teens, and adults who are supporting each other, talking each other down from suicide with poems and videos, or helping each other with schoolwork or personal problems. We don't pay attention to the millions of people of all ages making positive videos and sharing what they're passionate about. There is a new type of community forming, and our kids are growing up as founding members.

This is some of the good that can come from being online. Yes, there are bullies. Yes, there are online predators. Yes, there is a darker side to the Internet. But kids are getting online anyway, so doesn't it make sense to find ways to support them, help them navigate and avoid the darker aspects, and celebrate all the amazing things they're doing? Like all of us, they are looking for approval, for someone to say they've done well. They get that approval from their community, should they not get it from their families as well?

So when I hear from teens that they don't want to tell their parents what they're up to because they're afraid their parents won't understand or, worse, will take what is important to them and use it to control them, it both breaks my heart and makes me want to show the world what is going on. Our children deserve the support and recognition they seek from their families.

We worry about letting our kids online, and rightfully so. The Internet can be a scary place, and we should be wary of it. But it's far better to educate our children and keep communication open than to simply deny them that which they desire the most.

Kids are smart. Really smart. Talk to a group of kids, and you'll find that they likely know more than most adults about protecting themselves online and safeguarding their information. They help each other learn tricks to stay safe. They know about making secure passwords, and false identities with alternate names and birthdays.

They know how to discourage uncomfortable questions and how to let adults know that something is amiss. They police themselves, and they do a good job at it. So maybe we need to let them know we trust them and that there is good happening. We need to make sure they have the tools and support they need so they don't have to figure it out for themselves or feel that they need to hide their online activities from their parents.

ONLINE SAFETY

Being online can open many doors, but we must provide our children with the information they need to navigate those waters. As parents, we want to protect our children, provide them with the best opportunities, and give them options that will help them grow and learn. We research the best schools, put them in extracurricular classes, encourage them to be healthy and fit, and make sure they experience the natural world. So of course we want to monitor what they're doing online to ensure that they make good, safe choices.

The Internet is a big, mysterious, ever-changing environment. For parents who aren't online very much, it is the unknown. It can be harder to monitor what kids are doing online than what they're watching on TV. We use programs to make sure they're not going to inappropriate sites, we restrict their access to the Internet, and we work on controlling what they do and see. But we often neglect to teach them what to do when they find their way to sites they shouldn't, how to present themselves safely to others in ways that won't divulge personal information, how to trust their gut when they need to, or when to let an adult know that something doesn't feel right. Teaching kids these skills, which I'll cover in Chapter 8, is at least as important as shielding them is.

COMMUNICATION AND TRUST

There are a few things we can do to make sure our kids are safer online, but the most fundamental one of all is to communicate with them. This isn't as simple as it might seem. At the root of open communication is trust, and that runs both ways. You need to have faith in your child, in their ability to make wise decisions, and in their choices of behavior. And your children need to trust you. They need to know that they can come to you with any issue without fear of being ridiculed, overly questioned, or shut down. It takes time to build trust if it has been lacking on either side.

 Trust in Cori's House

THIS IS A COMPLETELY PERSONAL take on parenting, how I have raised Xander, and how I treat every child in my care, no matter their age or their personality—it fits the wilder, more independent kids as much as it does the easy going, happy-to-please ones. It's also how every mentor I've truly admired has behaved with children. This approach is based on respect, trust, and responsibility.

My underlying belief is that every person deserves to be treated with respect and dignity, from a toddler having a tantrum to a senior facing losing their driver's license. Starting with that as a foundation means I do my best to treat people the way I want to be treated. It also means that I expect that they are fully capable of acting in a responsible and trustworthy way—suited to their age and abilities, of course.

We're all human and we all lose our cool sometimes, but it is rare for me to raise my voice or speak in anger. I don't mock or ridicule, and I try hard to see things from the child's point of view. Have I always been like this? Absolutely not. It took years of learning about myself and learning not to be overly controlling or reactive. I learned from mentors, from my own experiences, and most of all from kids. I wouldn't want someone to ridicule or yell at me, so why would I feel I have the right to do that to someone else, especially someone as powerless as a child?

Trust in Cori's House *(continued)*

At the same time, I will not accept being treated poorly by anyone, including children. I expect the same respect I give. And that may take a while to gain, but when we reach a point of mutual trust, things become much easier and smoother, and life becomes more fun. I've spent almost half my life working with kids with a variety of acting-out behaviors, in settings from day-cares to schools to a psychiatric hospital, so I've had my patience tried many a time. And in almost all those cases, mutual respect and trust have been the foundation for success.

When it comes to trust, my approach is twofold. I show that I can be trusted, and I demonstrate my trust for others. I do my best not to make promises I cannot keep and to be as reliable and predictable as I can be. And when I mess up, I take responsibility and apologize. I'm only human, and that's part of the learning process too. Some-times things happen, but if I say I'm going to do something, I do my absolute best to make it happen. This means I can't make sweeping declarations of things I can't guarantee, but it also means that I can be counted on, and kids slowly learn that.

Extending trust is a little more calculated. I want to encourage trustworthy behaviors, and I want the behav-ior to come from within, not from a fear of punishment or a desire to please. In our house, and with the kids I work with, trustworthiness is directly tied to privileges and responsibilities. I don't want kids to have to push at bound-aries that are unfair or overly restrictive; I want to change and relax those boundaries as soon as I know I can trust the kids, often before they're even aware that there was a boundary to push. That way, they know I have greater (and real) trust in them.

Trust in Cori's House *(continued)*

As Xander has gotten older, rules and boundaries have shifted and changed. Since we homeschool, he can sleep in, so I let him stay up late. He monitors and takes responsibility for being rested the next day; if he knows we have an early activity he heads to bed earlier—most of the time. And the times he doesn't, he learns from the experience. He also learns that while I might be sympathetic, it won't earn him a reprieve from activities or work. This might sound unstructured and as if I have no rules at all, but nothing could be further from the truth. I can be strict, and I have clear expectations. I just don't have rules that are unnecessary or unfair.

The same thing goes for being online. I trust Xander, and he knows it. We don't have privacy locks or child monitors on the computer. I don't check his history or chat logs. I give him his privacy, as that too is something he's earned. I know that if something makes him uncomfortable, he'll leave and he'll tell me about it. We've talked in detail about pretty much everything he might need to know about being online. Curiosity may overrule his common sense or his self-control at some point, but we'll deal with it—probably by talking about it, and possibly with a reasonable but clear consequence.

Trust is a two-way street, and through mutual trust and respect, we can have open communication. His trust extends not just to knowing I'll be fair with boundaries but also to knowing that I will respect him and listen to his views. And that means he can tell me things without fear of unfair reprisal. And I can trust him to talk to me and share things, which means I have fewer worries about what he's doing.

The deal with all of this, though, is that it needs to be genuine. Your children will know if you're not being real with them, and that will cause them to distrust you more. That distrust leads to hiding things, not fully sharing information, or leading a secret life. The bottom line is that we want our children and teens to *want* to let us know if something isn't going well or if they're excited for something or about pretty much anything they care to discuss. It really will help them be safer online if they're not hiding anything from you.

■ WHEN TRUST NEEDS TO BE ESTABLISHED

Not all children can earn trust quickly. Some have learned sneaky behaviors that they need to unlearn. Some like to challenge the rules and push the boundaries, no matter how far you extend them, and some are simply impulsive and need more support to learn how to make better choices. In these situations, it makes sense to start with very tight rules and expectations and then loosen them as your kids prove they can handle the responsibility.

Within their abilities, all kids can follow guidelines and rules, make respectful choices, and be counted on. But we're all different, and two children from the same family who were raised with the same values and parenting can still be completely different. For example, you may have a child who struggles with impulse control and forgets the rules, or one who loves to argue and always believes she is right. In these cases, as in every case, you need to work with the child to make sure he can be successful at making better choices. What works for one child may not for the other, and that is OK. Rules don't need to be the same across the board, nor do consequences. What reinforces one child may make no difference to another. They learn that you will address their needs, support them, and provide consequences that are specific to each child.

In the case of an impulsive child, this might mean keeping the computer where you can always see it or allowing your child to use the computer only if you are beside them. This can be frustrating, but hopefully your child will respond well, and such rigid boundaries can slowly be lifted. Extend their privileges and boundaries when they have earned it. If they backslide, tighten your controls and rule.

With older kids who deliberately challenge you by sneaking online later than agreed or pushing the boundaries in other ways, you may need to remove computer access completely. If this interferes with their homework, you can put limits on the time they spend on a game or online. Communicate with your kids, and find out why they are so determined to be online at a certain time or what is worth arguing so strongly for. There may be people waiting for them to finish a project or go on a raid. They may have made a commitment to viewers wanting to watch them stream. They may have set a personal goal they want to meet. If you can get a sense of what their goals are, perhaps you can meet at a middle ground. I do not mean caving in to their demands, but if something is vitally important to your child, even if you can't see it yourself, it still tells you a lot about them. It isn't fair to use this information against them as punishment. Use the information to come up with a plan that will benefit everyone.

If playing games is causing nothing but stress, there is always the option to uninstall the game and walk away for a bit, though this is bound to cause more trouble than it solves. Try to find more positive ways to work with your child, and avoid all-or-nothing gestures that are sure to cause disagreement.

ONLINE PRIVACY

We should be teaching our children about online privacy before they ever log on. These are the same basic rules we teach kids about talking to strangers: Don't give out personal information, such as your real name, your age, or where you live (especially your address). Xander and I play Minecraft with players around the world, so we disclose a general area but not precisely where we're from. We might say we live on the West Coast, without specifying the country. Or we might say we're from Canada, BC, or even Vancouver Island. On the main server we play on, people know we're from Victoria, which is fine with me, but on other servers I'd never disclose that much. Giving a region or even a time zone can be more than enough. Tell your children in advance how you want them to answer the question of where they're from. You can even post it near the computer.

Decide what is comfortable for your family and talk about it. While you're on the topic of privacy, discuss peer pressure, stranger danger, what you want your kids to do if they're feeling bullied or uncomfortable, and how you want them to respond if someone wants their personal information. You want them to learn how to handle simple issues on their own. You may want them to handle things by ignoring the person bothering them or by seeking help on the server they are on. Your own family rules will dictate their answers, but if your children don't know what your wishes and expectations are, they may not answer in a way you'd like. Ensure that they know in advance.

No matter what the situation, you want your children to share it with you, if only so you can debrief them and, hopefully, compliment them on how they handled it. You can also provide suggestions for how to approach a similar situation in the future, and you can follow up on your own if need be. Communication and trust are key. If your children don't feel that they can approach you, they won't.

▧ PAY ATTENTION

Keep computers in a shared family space. Pay attention to what your kids are doing, and ask them to share their work with you. Get to know their online friends a bit, and say hi to them through your child. I'm not suggesting you lurk over your kids' shoulders, unless they've not earned enough trust for you to give them some space and privacy, but I do suggest you keep an eye open and be available if something should go awry.

THE MINECRAFT CONNECTION

What does this have to do with Minecraft? After all, you can play it as a single-player game, or you can set up a home server and invite only people you know to join it. Your children don't ever need to be online, right?

This is all true, but what if your children could use Minecraft as a way to safely explore what the Internet has to offer? It is very likely that at some point your child will want to explore other servers and play other games. They'll want to explore online videos and join groups and activities.

Wouldn't it be better to help them navigate those online realms when they're young enough to listen to you? It will happen well before your kids are teens—no matter the boundaries you impose, they will find ways to be online. And if you haven't established trust and built foundations for communication and online safety before then, you may never know what they're doing. If you can meet them partway, you can ensure that they have the social and emotional skills they need to navigate online.

The best way to do this is to play together, or at the very least to spend time actively participating when your child is online. When Xander first wanted to join a server, at the age of 11, I was terrified. I wanted to know who he was going to be hanging out with, why these people wanted to spend so much time online, and what they could possibly be doing. And remember, I was a gamer mom who was pretty online savvy, and Xander and I have a very good relationship, including ample trust and communication, so for me to be so worried is saying something.

My solution was to make sure that I was around when he was online, and that the other players knew that I was. Our main computer has always been in the living room, so it was easy enough for me to hang out with Xander when he went online. I went in expecting the worst, but what happened surprised me. All the players invited me in and included me, even though I wasn't playing. They would ask Xander if his mom was there, and they would say hi to me. They'd show me their skins (their character appearance) or have Xander follow them in the game so they could give me tours of their builds. They welcomed him with open arms, and they helped him learn the rules and etiquette of playing on their server.

Bit by bit my fears were laid to rest. As Xander learned the ropes, I was there alongside him, letting him figure things out but being there when he was frustrated or needed support. As he became savvier and I became more comfortable with the server and how he was managing on it, I was able to pull back and allow him more freedom.

 ## Wrednax

BACK WHEN I FIRST JOINED the server, I started a small town with a partner. Knowing nothing about how to actually make a town, we didn't use any of the protective mechanisms to defend it, and an enemy player took over the base for two hours before we fought him off.

I slowly learned how to defend my base with the help of other people on the server. Even with the help, I was tricked and raided from within by town members, and I had to learn who to trust.

GROWING WITH MINECRAFT

Minecraft can be adapted not only to suit your family's beliefs and rules about gaming but also to suit your children as they grow more mature and experienced, something that is rare to find in a game.

CHOOSING SETTINGS

It is easy to start with peaceful, creative settings and then slowly change them as your child is ready. Age doesn't necessarily make the best marker in such things—consider your child's personality and maturity level, as well as your own values and beliefs. If you know that your child is likely to be devastated if a creeper destroys his house, keep him on Peaceful. If you have an intrepid explorer, let her try a survival map. You don't need the same rules for every child. And you can always change things as they grow more experienced.

EXPANDING BOUNDARIES

I find that if I am able to extend a child privileges as acknowledgment of their being responsible and trustworthy, they are more likely to continue to be responsible and trustworthy. I'm not talking about bribes or rewards. I don't make a big deal of it, except maybe to explain why they can now play a different level, stay up later, or have more computer time. I don't remove computer privileges as a consequence, unless it is directly related, because that is usually punitive and likely to cause resentment rather than a change in behavior.

FAMILY-FRIENDLY SERVERS

Many servers are family friendly, with programming that blocks rude language and staff that monitor for appropriateness. Some servers make sure that kids have positive experiences and that they never lose their hard-earned items. Others are more relaxed, and kids will sometimes have to deal with their work being destroyed (*griefed*, in Minecraft language) or their items stolen in raids. Depending on the age, temperament, and personality of the child, some servers may be a better fit than others. A simple online search will give a lot of information about servers, and we'll explore them in Chapter 8.

HOUSE RULES

Chances are you already have some house rules in place. Families with more than one child are familiar with the dynamics and challenges of ensuring that everyone takes turns. Involving the entire family in making the rules will allow children to have some ownership, whether there is a single child or many.

You might consider drawing up a contract that everyone must sign and abide by (see the Appendix for a sample contract), creating a schedule (and posting it somewhere visible to everyone), and using a timer to track turn length. Setting predictable and consistent days or hours and sticking with them will allow children to plan their time. Remember that this, like all play, is their work; children are constantly learning and growing as they play. When it comes to Minecraft, they may have responsibilities to others if they are playing on a server, and very likely they have personal goals they wish to achieve. External cues such as schedules and timers help children learn to organize their time. It's not a bad thing to introduce them to the idea of planning ahead. It is also helpful to include them in this planning, allow them to negotiate, and let them know that their voices carry some weight and that you respect their input. Of course your say will be the final one, and it's never a good idea to cave to kids' demands, but working together to find mutually acceptable guidelines is a great skill—this is perfect practice.

Cues can also be helpful in reminding kids when their time is nearing a close. Giving them a ten-minute warning allows them to wind down whatever they are working on. Minecraft projects can be big and involved, and sometimes it's very hard to walk away from a project that is almost complete. Here, consistency is key. If their time is up, and you don't want fights daily, don't give them wiggle room. Wiggle room teaches children that sometimes you'll give in, and so they should fuss and argue on the off chance that this is one of those times. I'm not saying don't give them extra time now and again, but let them barter for it by trading in some of their next time or by earning it with chores. Or use it as a reward. Be creative with that extra time—your kids value it. At the same time, don't use it for punishment that isn't related to playing or online time. That just builds resentment and erodes trust.

There are as many ways to monitor and plan online time as there are families. Use your best judgment, but be willing to be flexible if your plans need to change. And remember that you can use your kids' online time to connect with them. Have them show you what they're working on or teach you something about the game. Or get your own account and play on another computer on the same server as them. Have fun sharing this time with them, even just every now and then.

A WORD ON ADDICTION

Like many other things in life, gaming can be addictive. You set goals, meet them, and feel successful, so you want to repeat that action. There are many jobs and activities in Minecraft, and it is eminently satisfying and inherently rewarding to complete them.

Mining is a prime example: You mine for blocks, finding coal and iron, sometimes redstone, or even lapis lazuli, but none of these ores are rare. Then you see a blue shimmer—diamond! It is like hitting the jackpot at a casino. Instant reward, and suddenly the past 15 minutes spent mining seems like nothing, and you're eager to continue.

This intrinsic reward—combined with the pride of finishing a build or succeeding in a raid—makes Minecraft enticing, to say the least. Being able to play with friends, discuss the game at school, or share your work online in videos adds to its draw.

I'm a firm believer in educating kids rather than laying out rules. If they are showing signs that they are addicted to the game, by all means limit their time and help them find ways to balance their lives. Encourage other activities, both physical and creative. Suggest other outlets, provide opportunities to be active, and give them art supplies. But at the same time, teach them about why it's addictive. Use this as a chance to open a dialogue with them so they can learn to monitor themselves. Use visual schedules and timers, help them learn to use those tools on their own, and empower them to take control of their time management. This is tricky, so they will need your positive support.

BEHAVIOR CONCERNS

If Minecraft causes too much drama in your house—if your kids are fighting, getting overly upset about having to log off when their turn is done, or reacting strongly to things happening within the game—you may need to have them take a break. Or you might need to revisit your house rules or create new ones to address the issues. Whatever you do, communicate with your children, tell them your concerns, and listen to them as well. Sometimes what seem like issues of addiction to the game are actually far simpler.

For example, if your child isn't being given fair warning that their time is almost over, they may be in the middle of something in the game that they legitimately cannot walk away from without consequence. Remember that it is important to them. If you were asked to walk away from a task without time to finish, you too might be frustrated, even if it were just a recreational activity. In such a situation, you might be able to come to an easy compromise—you might give them a warning or use a timer. You'll find that your child is able to transition away from playing with ease.

But I never advocate giving in to a tantrum, drama, pleading, or whining. This is another type of reinforcement, and if your child succeeds once, they will try again and again until they succeed. This is easier said than done, but being clear and consistent in the moment and taking steps to avoid a repetition (making clear rules, involving your child once he is calm) will go a long way to stopping these behaviors and make everyone feel more at ease. Knowing the expectations eases anxiety for everyone, not just children, and can help keep peace in your home.

BALANCE

There is a time and place for all things, including technology and gaming. Finding a balance that works for your family may take a while, but it will be worth it. Find ways to share technology with your children, be it through games, the Internet, videos, or other ways. They may surprise you with the things they know.

Use scheduling Minecraft to jump-start other activities, such as going for a walk or swim. If you have more than one child, read or have quiet time with the child who is not taking a turn playing Minecraft. Time Minecraft turns to coincide with busy times, such as when you're making dinner. Different times might work best for different personalities, so pay attention to their rhythms and needs.

Rather than remove earned privileges, I try to find suitable consequences, and I reward positive choices with an extra five minutes of play time or activity.

Finally, try to relax about screen time. Be aware of the amount of time you spend on screens, what you're modeling for your kids, and the reality that we all enjoy time on screens. As long as you're open to the possibilities, Minecraft can be an amazing addition to family activities.

MANAGING RISING EMOTIONS

We are emotional beings with a full range of feelings, and as we get older, we learn to control those emotions and our responses to things that might stimulate them. For example, we might feel disappointment when learning that we've run out of our favorite snack. We might express that disappointment with a sigh, a groan, shutting a cupboard door a bit harder than necessary, or finding someone in the house to point an accusatory finger at. But we have learned to moderate our responses and to develop emotional resiliency.

Now think about a small child who discovers that her favorite snack is unavailable. Chances are good that the reaction will be larger. There could be tears, screaming, or kicking. And if there are other factors in play, such as hunger or exhaustion, the response is likely to be swifter and more volatile.

Older children face the same challenges in regulating their emotions, though the triggers might be different. Losing (or winning) a game often brings up a plethora of emotions. As we mature, we all learn to moderate and control those feelings, predict when we might experience them, and find socially acceptable ways to deal with them. Those years of learning are tricky. We're learning so much more at the same time, and we're developing physically, socially, and intellectually. And just when things start to come together, our hormones kick in and we can find ourselves right back where we were as toddlers, wanting instant gratification and not being able to cope with disappointment.

Thankfully, those years pass, though not quickly enough for many of us. Life becomes smoother if we can remember what is happening and find ways to address emotional responses. Parents can learn what the triggers are and pass that knowledge on to kids to enable them to understand what is going on and take some control.

We don't need to remove the triggers completely or cater to our children to avoid emotional outbursts. We just need to use our knowledge to avoid setting our children up for failure. This will help them learn to deal with disappointment and frustration.

▨ EMOTIONAL RESILIENCY

Emotional resiliency is the ability to bounce back from frustration or disappointment, work through sadness or jealousy, and moderate emotions. It is a skill that needs to be developed. In some ways, it develops on its own as we learn to cope with negative experiences and manage positive ones. We learn not to be overcome with excitement or swept completely away by new love. But other factors come into play, and they can make our emotions more difficult to regulate and process.

Even when our kids are very young, we can start teaching them about emotions. The easiest way to do this is to name what they are experiencing as it's happening, so that they know what it is. You can do this gently without upsetting them, though sometimes when we feel we're being understood, our first reaction is an extra wave of emotion—at last someone understands! So for that sad toddler denied their snack, you can say, "Oh that's frustrating. You really wanted that cookie" or "How disappointing. I'm sorry, but the cookies are all gone." You are naming the emotion, and you're saying it's OK to have it.

What you're not doing is trying to stop the emotion in the moment. Eventually you might need to help your child move through their upset and carry on with their day, through distraction or a change in scenery. But in the moment, you can support them by calmly empathizing with them while at the same time not rescuing them from the emotion or denying their right to experience it. Often that is enough to stop the storm in its tracks.

As a parent, you'll know when to step in and when to hold back. No one knows your young child as well as you do. With consistency and calmness, teach your child that emotions are OK and that they can manage and control them.

As your child grows older, expand your conversations. Talk about what caused an emotional reaction, and explain that we can feel multiple emotions at once. If your child already has the vocabulary, talking about things is much easier. Introduce the idea of how to manage their emotions. Teach them the value of a deep breath or three, or of walking away from a frustrating situation. Help them learn to express themselves and let someone know how they are feeling. By allowing them to honestly own those emotions, you're letting them know you have faith in their ability to experience and manage them.

Letting kids know that it's OK to cry can be a challenge. We don't like to see someone in distress, and we want it to end quickly. Sometimes we tell children to deny their emotions or to convert them (for instance, turning tears to anger). This won't create emotional resiliency, though it might appear that the child is in control of his emotions. Instead, the child learns that emotions are something to be ashamed of, to be hidden. Suppressing emotions can lead to unexpected outbursts, negative self-talk, and children who feel they need to hide a part of themselves from the people around them.

Giving children a voice and empowering them is a better choice. Those tears can be a strength because they work as a pressure valve, allowing them to process and work through emotions before releasing them.

Now is also the time to start teaching your child about the effect of outside factors on their emotional well-being. When they're being overly cranky, ask them (politely!) when and what they last ate. When you overreact because you haven't eaten and your blood sugar levels are down, explain it to them. Don't use it as an excuse. Own your actions and behaviors, and explain them rather than making excuses for them.

If your child is overtired and therefore weepy, hyper, or cuddly, discuss it with them. Ask them how they feel when they don't have adequate sleep compared to when they do. No matter how we enforce bedtimes, there will always be unexpected late nights or broken sleep. And sleepiness definitely affects our actions and reactions.

As your child approaches her teen years, surges in hormones complicate matters. Suddenly something that would never have fazed them is overwhelming and devastating. Or they become giddy and silly to a point that seems completely out of control. Rather than ignoring or brushing off these changes, accept them as a real and confusing part of growing up, and help your pre-teen or teen understand what is happening. Explore what happens when they have rapid growth spurts or when hormones surge and peak. There is nothing to be embarrassed by or kept secret here—knowledge is power for everyone involved.

From the time Xander was young, I've always made a point of talking about things. We got a lot of the potentially embarrassing conversations out of the way before he was old enough to know he should be embarrassed. And while there are subjects that aren't easy to discuss, I know that we'll avoid a lot of confusion or miscommunication when we do.

I refuse to see hormones as an excuse for any behavior or action, though I know there are different philosophies on this. At the same time, I cannot ignore the fact that for a day or two every month I might be weepier, quicker to lose control, and more insecure. So I try to avoid challenging situations, and I try to be a little gentler on myself. I've let Xander know that it is a part of life, and something I am neither ashamed of nor hiding behind.

So when Xander started to become more teary, more emotional, and quicker to anger, I asked if he thought some of his reactions were hormonal, and he thought about it and agreed that they were. From there we discussed how to handle it. He's learned that there are times when it isn't wise to engage in a debate online, for instance, or try a new game that will frustrate him; he waits until he's in a better emotional state. And he agreed that I could use him as an example in this book, hoping it might help other kids understand themselves.

EMOTIONS AND GAMING

From the moment a child wakes till you're tucking them in, they're experiencing the full gamut of emotions, and it's easy to find times when they can be commended for handling a situation calmly or encouraged to take a deep breath. And video games, which often challenge us to the point of frustration, are another source of teachable moments.

Video games, by their very structure, are designed to push players to achieve higher and higher goals. Many games combine puzzles and physical coordination to challenge the player. By playing successively more difficult levels, players develop skills and gain knowledge that will help them advance. But it is exceedingly rare for a gamer to run through a game without facing frustrations and challenges. Sometimes the frustration is so great that the player needs to quit. Choosing to quit when things get frustrating is actually a skill. Many people struggle with this and will play to the point of sheer anger, resulting in what in gaming terms is aptly known as *rage quitting*.

This may sound counterproductive or alarming, but it's not. The linear structure of many games is such that it develops goal setting and includes intrinsic rewards as the game progresses. This allows players to feel positive and want to continue in the face of frustration and challenge. Encouraging kids not to quit any activity is a good thing. But games are more complex than we realize at first glance, and managing emotion with respect to games is one aspect of this.

MANAGING GAMING EMOTIONS

Minecraft combines intellectual skills with fine motor-physical challenges. But unlike linear games, it is not designed to become progressively more challenging. Its greatest frustrations often occur when players are first learning how to play. They are learning not only how to craft and build but how to fight monsters, especially those dreadful creepers that destroy a player's hard work. Gamers need to figure out all the steps themselves—there are no helpful tutorials—and they often learn through failure.

Combine these challenges with the excitement of an unrestricted world, in which players can create virtually anything they can imagine, and you have a game that can be enjoyable and emotionally rewarding as well as frustrating and even devastating. Now imagine an emotionally volatile young person (or perhaps a calm and even-tempered one) sitting down to play. They are starting to figure things out, and then suddenly there is a hissing sound and an explosion, and all their work is lost. Or they fall into a pool of lava and all their found items are destroyed. The impact can be more frustrating than you'd think, especially if they've been working on something a long time and see the fruits of their efforts damaged or destroyed.

Such challenges are minimal when playing on Creative mode, but eventually almost every child wants to try their hand at Survival mode. And even with settings on Peaceful, things will happen. Your child might go searching for resources and get lost and never find their home again, particularly if they built far from their spawn point. I can speak from experience, as I had no idea how easy it is to get turned around. And I regularly get lost to this very day, much to my gaming partners' chagrin and entertainment (**Figure 3.1**).

FIGURE 3.1 Even with a map and a partner, it's still possible to get lost!

▓ REDUCING FRUSTRATION

Every player new to Minecraft will experience certain challenges. While I don't believe in rescuing kids from every frustrating or challenging situation, there are times when it's in their best interests to intervene. Older players, used to video games, may well be able to predict these challenges and avoid or mitigate them, but even they can be faced with enough frustration to cause them to walk away. Younger players, some of whom have never played anything more than simple games on a tablet, can find these challenges frustrating.

Many children are determined to work on their own and will not take advice. Others may be devastated and demand you fix the problem. And sadly, sometimes that is not possible. And while your quick response might be "this is just a game," remember that for your children it is their work, and it might be work that they've spent hours on. Dismissing or belittling their reactions will create a divide rather than a bond. At the very least, be there to listen and commiserate, even if there is little else you can do.

With awareness, these challenges can sometimes be prevented or at least lessened. It's good for kids to know this, though many need to find out the hard way. The following three sections cover challenges that are likely to happen to new players.

GETTING LOST

This happens more quickly than you'd think. Maps are massive, and it's easy to get turned around. The simplest solution is to use a map mod like Rei's Minimaps (see Chapter 8), but most gamers will be impatient to get started. Pressing F3 (at the top of your keyboard) will display a variety of information, including your coordinates, but for new players this too can be confusing. When you're starting out, it is far simpler to use markers to create a path as you explore.

Some players make a path as they go, or they leave blocks or torches (if they are able to find coal) along their trail as markers.

Torches are the best markers. They show your path at night as well as during the day and are equally effective in mines. If torches aren't a possibility, then placing blocks of dirt or stone or any other material works, as does digging out a block every few steps. Make sure markers are close enough together that you can see the next one on the path before you lose sight of the previous one. As players become more adept and gather more materials, they can build paths as they proceed, though they may find that they don't get lost as easily once they become comfortable with the terrain.

If your child gets lost in the game and is trying to find their way home, have them stop right where they are and look for landmarks. When emotions are high, we tend to stop thinking clearly—this is as true in games as anything else. If nothing looks familiar, they can seek higher ground if it is nearby, or they can carefully *tower up*—building a tower of single blocks by jumping and placing a block underneath themselves—until they are high enough to see the surrounding landscape. If they jump or fall from their tower, chances are high that their character will die, so they will need to dig down through the tower to descend.

SUDDEN DEATH

There is nothing quite so frustrating as mining for diamonds or other ores and falling into lava with a full inventory of tools and items. A player can also die by accidentally mining gravel or sand and being smothered in a rockslide, by drowning, by falling, or by being killed by an attacking mob. When you die, you lose all the items in your inventory, as well as any armor you're wearing and any objects in your hand. You will return to your spawn point or your bed (if you made one), but your items will stay at your death point.

When you're starting a new game, it is a good idea to build a home near the spawn point where you joined the game. That way, if you die you will respawn at the same point and be close to home. If you build far from your spawn point, it is a good idea to make a bed and sleep in it. The bed will become your new spawn point, and you will return there if you die (but as always, without your items).

It is only sometimes possible to recover items. Items dropped in lava burn immediately. Items buried in stone disappear, though if you're close to a wall they will sometimes appear on the other side of the wall. Items dropped during a mob attack or in water, however, will remain where they were dropped for five minutes. If you can recall the precise place of death, you might be able to find your items.

Losing items can be extremely frustrating to a player, especially if they are carrying rare or valuable materials. If your child is distraught or frustrated, help them try to find their items, but let them know that they may have disappeared. There is no way to retrieve lost items. This is part of the risk of playing Minecraft, and your children will need to accept it if they are playing on a survival map. If they really struggle with this—deaths happen frequently when you first start playing Minecraft—they may need to consider playing on Creative mode for a while longer. Some kids find that after a taste of Survival they much prefer Creative, where they won't need to worry about such things.

For children who want to remain on a survival map, you can turn the game to Peaceful mode, which doesn't contain monsters but does contain the other ways to die. Hostile mobs appear only at night, so your kids can work during the Minecraft days and then hide somewhere protected and well lit at night. It is best to store valuables in a chest rather than carrying them.

CREEPER EXPLOSIONS

Another truly frustrating experience is loss through creeper explosions. Creepers, those green-moving bushes, follow a player. When one gets within a block of a player, it begins to hiss, which is a warning that it will explode in 1.5 seconds. It is possible to dodge out of the way of a creeper explosion, but they can still do extensive damage to the surrounding area. Like all mobs, they come out only at night.

If your child is working on a project, they need to be vigilant about the time of day in the game and seek shelter at night. If the volume is on, they can listen for the telltale signs of a creeper about to explode and run away from their work, but if they are too slow they might die or lose part of their build.

HELPING YOUR CHILD LEAD THE WAY

Despite warnings of game addiction, too much screen time, and potential dangers, technology and gaming have countless positive aspects. From encouraging problem-solving and communication to fostering learning, creativity, and emotional resiliency, games can have a place in our lives and the lives of our kids. Technology is moving into all facets of our lives, including the classroom, and kids are making the most of it.

In the past, gamers were seen as isolated and shut away from others. But now, online gaming communities, social media, and gaming conventions and meet-ups are bringing people together.

There are many ways to include games in your family routine. Playing together is one of the best ways to connect with kids, whether it's tossing a ball, playing a board game, or playing make-believe. Adding video games to the mix won't detract from those activities; it adds another way to spend time together. You have a chance to peek into your child's world and to join them in something they are passionate about.

The many learning opportunities offered by gaming are also not to be discounted, from increasing memory and processing speed to academics and creative thinking. Life skills such as problem solving and emotional resiliency are areas where gaming can help, and I don't mean only within the games, but also when planning how to make them fit into your lives.

Working together as a family to create and maintain balance is key. Showing respect for each other, communicating needs, coming up with a schedule that works with your family, and spending time discussing games are great learning moments. In Minecraft, the opportunities for creativity are limitless, and the ability to work together to make amazing projects can't be dismissed. Find that balance and pay attention to what your kids are doing, and you will likely find yourself delighted and awed by what unfolds.

GETTING STARTED

MINECRAFT IS VERY EASY to purchase. You can buy it online
from the Mojang website, or you can go directly to Minecraft.net
and buy it there (both end up in the same place, but the
Minecraft.net route eliminates several steps). Alternatively,
you can buy a gift card, available at many retailers, and
then use it to purchase your game. You can also buy a
Minecraft account for another person and have it
emailed to them, or it can be sent to you so you can
gift it directly (**Figure 4.1**). We'll walk
through the entire process.

FIGURE 4.1 There are many ways to purchase Minecraft.

THINGS TO CONSIDER BEFORE YOU BUY

Before you purchase your account, there are some things you need to take into consideration, such as for whom you are purchasing the account, what access they will have, and how many individual accounts you'd like to get. The number of accounts is important, because once a single user has begun to invest in their Minecraft experience, they are unlikely to want anyone else to manipulate their account and, by extension, their Minecraft worlds. You also need to decide on a user-name, something that requires some forethought.

SEPARATE ACCOUNTS

If multiple players are going to be playing, either they can share an account (and therefore won't be able to play at the same time) or they each need their own account. Although you can create endless saved maps, you can play as only one character. If at all possible, buy a sepa-rate account for each player in your family. That way, everyone has their own identity.

Remember that single-player maps are saved to the computer they are played on, and therefore anyone logging on to that computer can access them. This means that individual accounts won't necessarily stop your children from interfering with each other's work. It's a good idea to establish clear house rules and consequences (see Chapter 3, "Fitting Minecraft Fit into Family").

Having separate accounts becomes more important when playing on a server, because it is confusing to others on the server if the person behind the username is constantly shifting. For instance, if Wrednax and I were to share an account, it would cause many challenges beyond not being able to play at the same time. We have very different interests when we play—he is much more interested in PVP than I am, and I tend to be the server "mom," sharing resources and helping new players get settled. If we had one account, other players wouldn't know which of us was logged on unless we clarified each time someone new joined, which could be confusing (and tedious). And if we were playing on a server that uses the Towny plugin (a special modification), we'd really have challenges. Towny lets players create and join towns, and it blocks other players from building or breaking blocks in those towns, which is valuable in terms of protecting your materials. Were we to share a username on the Rawcritics PVP map, however, only one of us could join the town of our choosing, because players can be members of only one town. And since Wrednax is mayor of a PVP town and I'm a member of the only neutral town on the server, that could cause challenges. On other servers, there would be the potential for similar challenges, perhaps with different plugins.

If you are uncertain whether your children will play Minecraft, or you'd just like to try it first, then a shared account will work, particularly if they are just playing on single-player maps. If you take this route, make sure you create a username that will fit your child or yourself, because usernames cannot be changed.

SELECTING A USERNAME

Although Mojang has said on its site that you might be able to change your username in the future, it is not possible at this time. So put thought and care into selecting one. With over 10 million games sold, picking a good, unique username can be a challenge.

You won't know if a name has been used before you try it during the registration process, so you should have a few names prepared. Otherwise, you might find yourself hastily selecting something you or your child will regret.

PRIVACY

When you're playing a single-player game at home or on a private server where you know all the players, your username doesn't really matter much. You could use your real name, and it would be fine. But as soon as you start playing with other people on public servers, privacy becomes much more important. For example, a personal name like Cori_Dusmann, or even CDusmann, would be too revealing, particularly for a child. Even using your child's first name might make you uncomfortable, and it is fairly uncommon to see proper names as usernames.

There are many nicknames and choices available, but you may need to be creative. Wrednax is Xander's name spelled backward—the W is the first letter of his last name. People occasionally figure it out, but there is nothing else revealing about it, so I was fine with his choice. It's been a good one, because it is short, simple, and easy to remember.

If you're concerned about your child being identified by gender, be sure to pick a gender-neutral name. Although it's beginning to change, girl gamers have traditionally had a harder time gaining respect. I've had few problems on Rawcritics, and the Minecraft realm is actually very open and unbiased (relatively speaking). On less family-friendly servers, though, I've occasionally had to ward off unwanted attention and have at times wished I'd chosen a less obviously feminine name.

KEEP IT SHORT

Keep usernames short, especially for younger children. Choose something that your child will remember and be able to spell easily. Short usernames are also helpful in that other players can talk to you without doing a lot of writing. For example, when you send someone a private message on a server, you need to enter their full username. Make it easy for others to communicate with you or your children, and select a shorter name. Also, many commands and actions require the entry of your name and sometimes multiple names. For example, the teleport command usually requires the entry of two names. And even with short names, players will probably shorten them further: Wrednax is usually called Wred, I'm known as Whimsey or Whims, and I'm lazy enough to shorten a friend's four-letter username to the first letter, J.

KEEP IT SIMPLE

Usernames can be clever and descriptive, and they can express something about the individual. Keep it simple and easy to remember. Long strings of letters or words can be hard to remember, and even if they have meaning to the user, other players may not bother with messaging.

Be sure that the name when shortened is acceptable to you and your child, because chances are high that your name will be with you for a very long time.

BE CREATIVE

Have fun creating a username. Putting two semi-random words together can result in a fun, easy, and unique name. An adjective and a noun, or a noun and a verb, can work well together. For example, PowerPop, AquaBlue, or GiddyFrog, which might be nicknamed (or nicked, in game language) either Giddy or Frog. Names can be playful or serious, witty or goofy.

Using an underscore (_) or spare letters can help make the name unique but still easy to remember, for example, Fruity_Galore. Some players use X or Xx to bracket their names; for instance, XxWhimseysgirlxX.

One way to generate some name ideas is to write down a list of adjectives and a list of nouns with your kids. Cut them out and put them in separate bags. Take turns drawing to create names, and make a list of the top ones. Remember that it's always good to have a few names when you start to make an account, in case your preferred name is taken.

CHOOSE A NAME THAT WILL LAST

Although Mojang has said they're working on a way to allow players to change usernames, it may not happen for a long time. Help your children, especially younger ones, select a name that they can be happy with longterm. If they make friendships outside the game, they may still be identified as that username, so it's important to select one that actually represents them. I often call Xander Wred, and he calls me Whims—our usernames have just become nicknames.

CREATING A PASSWORD

To sign in to Minecraft, you will be using a username or the email address linked to the account, as well as a password. It is important to create a password that combines letters and numbers and that is not simple to guess or too short. Create a password solely for your Mojang account, especially if children are going to be logging in on their own, because you cannot know how secure they might keep that password. Pick something that is not obvious or easily figured out—if you need it to be easy to remember, make it personal to you, but don't use birthdays, your address, your phone number, or anything that can be easily guessed.

PURCHASING MINECRAFT

If you are in the United States or Australia, using a gift card may be the easiest way to buy Minecraft. There is also the option of purchasing Minecraft directly online. For either option you need to create a Mojang account first. This is not your Minecraft game account, but an account with Mojang itself.

CREATING A MOJANG ACCOUNT

Creating a Mojang account is easy.

1. In a browser, go to www.minecraft.net (**Figure 4.2**).

FIGURE 4.2 The Minecraft home page

2. Click Register in the upper-right corner.

   You are taken to the page where you'll set up your Mojang account before you purchase the game (**Figure 4.3**).

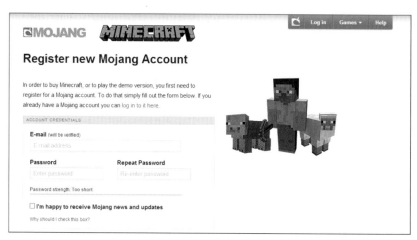

FIGURE 4.3 The Mojang account registration page

3. Enter your email address and password. Enter your password again in the Repeat Password field to verify they are identical. You will also be asked your name and birth date, as well as three security questions to verify your identity should you forget your password.

Note that children under the age of 13 must have a parent or guardian create an account for them (though this is something many kids get around simply by changing their age on the form).

You or your children will be using this email address to log on to Minecraft, so if you are planning to have more than one Minecraft account, you need to register for individual Mojang accounts as well.

Select the check box at the bottom of the page to accept Mojang's terms and conditions and privacy policy (links are available for both), and then click the Register button.

Once you enter your information, you are directed to a page stating that you have received a verification email.

4. Open the email verification. If you don't see the email in your inbox, look in your spam folder.

5. Click the link in the Mojang email, and a new page will open (**Figure 4.4**).

    This page has a clearly marked button for redeeming a prepaid gift card or gift code, but no immediately obvious place to actually purchase the game.

6. If you have a gift card or code, click the Redeem Gift Code or Prepaid Card button to go to the redemption page, and skip to the section "Creating Your Minecraft Game Profile." Otherwise, follow the directions in the next section, "Buying Minecraft Online."

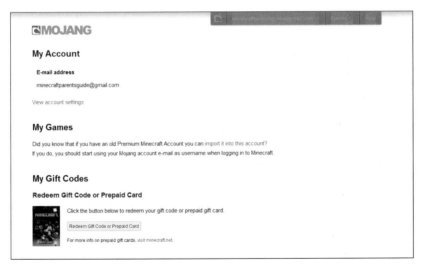

FIGURE 4.4 Your Mojang account page

BUYING MINECRAFT ONLINE

Buying the game is pretty straightforward. You will need a credit card or PayPal account, as well as your Mojang account information.

1. To get to Minecraft.net directly from the Mojang page where you created your account, click the drop-down menu in the upper right, hover your mouse pointer over Games, and then click Minecraft.

   or

   Go to www.minecraft.net in your browser.

   Now that you are registered, you will need to log in.

2. Click Log In in the upper-right corner, and you will be taken to a log-in page.

3. In the Username field, enter the email address you used to register, and enter your password in the field below that. New accounts with Mojang (since mid-2012) use an email address to log in.

4. Click the Buy Now button (**Figure 4.5**).

FIGURE 4.5 Buy it

You are redirected back to the Minecraft Store page (**Figure 4.6**). You'll see that the price is listed in Euros, but if you are in the United States, it will be converted to US dollars once you move through to the purchase page.

FIGURE 4.6 The Minecraft Store

5. Click "Buy Minecraft for this account."

On the purchase page, you will see the retail price, as well as a link to system recommendations (**Figure 4.7**). You'll also choose whether to buy the game for yourself or as a gift.

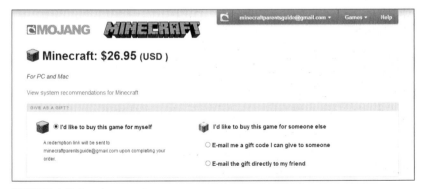

FIGURE 4.7 Purchase options

Your payment options list only Visa, MasterCard, and PayPal, but there is a more extensive list of options provided via the link below these choices.

6. Complete your billing address and make your payment type choice.

7. Click Proceed to Payment Details.

You are taken to a basic payment page.

8. Enter your billing information, and click Pay. You may be asked for a verification of your card. Follow the directions on your screen to complete your purchase.

When your purchase is complete, you are automatically directed to a page that gives you your receipt information and tells you that you must still choose a player name.

9. Click Check Your Inbox to be directed to an email that contains a link to the Create a Game Profile page and three links to download your new game for Windows, Mac, or Linux.

USING A GIFT CODE OR GIFT CARD

Redeeming a gift code or gift card is a matter of a few quick steps. Instructions are on the back of the gift card. In the US and Australia, cards can be purchased at many stores where gift cards are available. Mojang has announced that cards will soon be available in Canada and Europe but hasn't given a date for this.

1. Log in to your account at www.mojang.com. You will be taken to your account page (Figure 4.4).

2. Click the Redeem Gift Code or Prepaid Card button.

3. Enter your code, click the Redeem button, and you are ready to create your Minecraft profile.

CREATING YOUR MINECRAFT GAME PROFILE

Your game profile is where you select your username. It is also the place you need to go if you'd like to change your character's appearance (known as a *skin*) by uploading an image file (more on this later).

You can find the Create a Profile page at www.account.mojang.com. When you purchased the game, you were sent an email with a link to this page.

> **NOTE** You will not be using your username to log in to Minecraft. Rather, you will use the email address associated with your Mojang account.

1. Enter your username in the Profile Name field.

Remember that at this point, names cannot be changed, so be sure you are happy with your username.

2. Click Check Availability to see if your chosen name is available. If it is, click Choose Name. If your chosen name is not available, try another until you find a free name.

Once you've selected your name, you'll be asked if you are certain this is the choice you want.

3. Double-check the spelling, and be very sure before you proceed, because you will not be able to change it. Click the Choose Name button (**Figure 4.8**).

MOJANG

Create a game profile

Get going with Minecraft

Before you can start punching trees and what not, you first need to choose a name for your Minecraft profile. This name will be shown to other players that you meet in the game.

Choose a new name

You might not be able to change your name later, so please choose wisely!

Please note! When you **log in to Minecraft** or on minecraft.net, **use minecraftparentsguide@gmail.com** instead of the profile name that you choose below.

Profile name

Enter desired name   Check availability

Choose name

Use your registered Minecraft name

If you previously have registered for a free Minecraft account, you can use your existing username instead.

Use my existing Minecraft name

FIGURE 4.8 Creating a game profile

Your page updates, with your new account, its start date, and your username listed under the My Games section. Now you are ready to download Minecraft.

DOWNLOADING AND INSTALLING MINECRAFT

Once you have registered your game and set up an account, you can download and install Minecraft.

If you are not already logged in, log in to your Mojang account. You will find that Minecraft has been added under the My Games section, along with your start date, your profile name, and the download buttons for Windows, Mac, and Linux (**Figure 4.9**).

NOTE I've included the download directions for Windows and Mac. Linux users should search online if needing help.

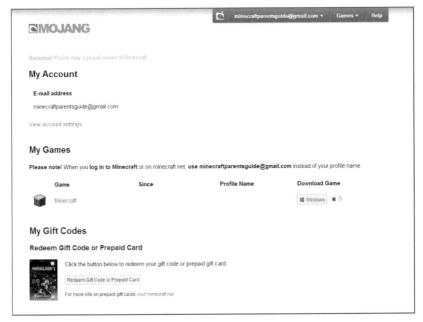

FIGURE 4.9 An updated accounts page with Minecraft included

WINDOWS

1. Click the Windows button under "Download Game."

Your computer downloads the Minecraft.exe file.

2. Save it where you wish; on your desktop or in a games folder, for example.

3. Double-click Minecraft.exe to run it.

Minecraft opens its launcher.

4. Enter your Mojang account email address (not your Minecraft username) and password.

5. Ignore the coding and tabs at the top, and click Play at the bottom of the page.

You'll find yourself at the Minecraft main menu, ready to play (**Figure 4.10**).

FIGURE 4.10 The Minecraft launch page

OS X

1. Click the Apple logo button under "Download Games." Minecraft downloads to your Downloads folder.

2. Drag Minecraft from the Downloads folder to your Applications folder.

3. Double-click the Minecraft icon.

4. Ignore the coding and tabs at the top, and press Play at the bottom of the page.

You'll find yourself at the Minecraft main menu, ready to play.

CHAPTER 5

SURVIVING YOUR FIRST NIGHT

IN CREATIVE MODE, there isn't a lot to learn other than how to place and remove blocks. There are no mobs. You have access to every item in the game, so there's no need to learn how to find or craft anything. You can fly and you cannot die, so you can build at any height. In short, you have complete freedom to do whatever you'd like, and there is no risk to experimenting.

Playing on Survival mode is a completely different matter, as its name attests. Even when playing on Survival mode's Peaceful setting with no monsters, you can still die from falls, drowning, lava, or even suffocation.

When you start a game on a survival map, there are no directions or tutorial. You find yourself spawned at a random location, and you need to figure out what to do. The game is not intuitive.

Surviving your first night can be a challenge. I'll take you through a typical first day and night on the Easy setting of a survival map, with tips to help you make it through.

TIP There are many videos on YouTube that also cover the first night, and it can be both entertaining and enlightening to watch some of them.

Don't worry about taking notes or remembering specific details here, this is just a sample run-through of a first night. I'll break everything down into very simple steps in the next chapter.

GAME SETTINGS

Minecraft provides settings that allow you to select the appropriate level of risk at which you or your child play, providing a challenge without excessive frustration.

- **Easy:** There are fewer mobs, but they can still kill you. You will drop to half your health (portrayed by a health meter bar of hearts) if you run out of food, but you won't starve.

- **Normal:** Monsters deal regular damage, and running out of food will leave you with half a heart in your health meter.

- **Hard:** Not only can you starve, but monsters deal more damage, and they are are more plentiful and more powerful.

Difficulty settings are managed in the Options menu within the game. You'll learn how to set them in the next chapter. For this walk-through, they're at the default setting, Normal.

GETTING STARTED

As we walk through the steps, you'll see that Minecraft is quite com-plex. You might feel a little overwhelmed—I did. But it isn't hard to learn, so let's get started.

■ CREATE A NEW WORLD

To start a new Survival game, open Minecraft and log in with your email address and password. When you click Play, the game loads and takes you to the main menu. From here, click Singleplayer (**Figure 5.1**).

FIGURE 5.1 The Minecraft start menu

A menu page provides you with options to play worlds you've already started as well as an option to create a new world. Click the Create New World button to display a screen on which you can name your world (**Figure 5.2**).

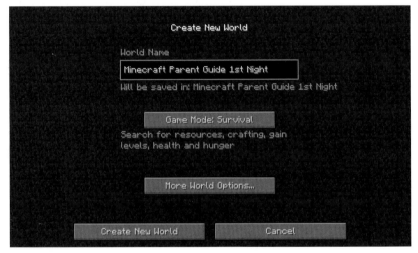

FIGURE 5.2 The Create New World menu is simple and straightforward.

The game mode is already set to Survival, so you can simply enter a name for your new world and click the Create New World button.

When you start your game, a new world map will generate randomly. You appear at your spawn point, which is where you will return if you die (minus any items you were carrying in your inventory). Your spawn point will never change, but you can create a new spawn point by crafting and sleeping in a bed. If your bed breaks, you end up back at this original spawn point.

When you log in to your new world, you see the game from a first-person perspective. You have an empty inventory—that's the bar at the bottom of your screen—as well as a full health meter, which is represented by hearts, and a full hunger bar, represented by little drumsticks. You will also see your arm on the screen—that's the blocky rectangle to the right of your inventory and meters (**Figure 5.3**).

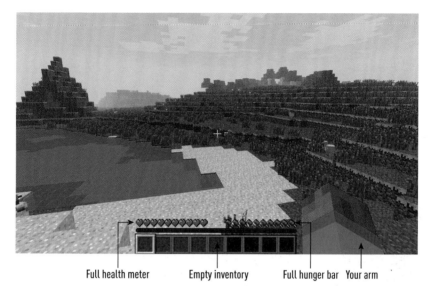

Full health meter   Empty inventory   Full hunger bar   Your arm

FIGURE 5.3 Your inventory, your health and hunger meters, and your arm

■ SPAWN POINT

At your spawn point, you don't have much but your full health and hunger meters. Time to start exploring!

In this game, I have spawned by a beach. I can see birch, oak, and spruce trees close-by, so there is ample wood to make tools. I also see several chickens, so I won't have to look hard for food.

■ MAKING TOOLS

My priorities are to get food and make a shelter. Since I see chickens close-by, I know I have access to food. Now I need a way to get that food.

This is where some players get squeamish. Although I could look for wheat to make bread, wheat needs to be planted from grass seeds and grow before it can be harvested, so I shall have to go hunting. When I'm hunting, I could hit a chicken repeatedly, but it is much faster to kill it with a sword. Time to make some tools!

STEP 1: HARVEST WOOD

Move toward a tree using the keyboard; this is not intuitive to first-time computer gamers, so I will explain how in the next chapter. For now, follow me as I approach a tree and punch it. Yes, you read that right. I punch a tree or two and collect some wood (**Figure 5.4**).

Birch tree   Birch tree block   Arm

FIGURE 5.4 Punching a birch tree to acquire wood

STEP 2: MAKE A CRAFTING BENCH

To craft objects, such as tools, I need to use some of my harvested wood to make a crafting bench (also called a crafting table). Pressing the letter E on my keyboard opens my inventory (**Figure 5.5**). All the parts of the inventory are explained in detail in Chapter 6—for now, you can see that I have logs from the two trees I knocked down (six blocks each of birch and oak, as indicated by the numbers on the logs in my grid) and one sapling, which I can plant to grow a new tree. Also on my inventory screen are four slots for armor (which I can craft from leather, iron, gold, or diamond), a grid of 27 empty blocks for items I acquire, and a bottom row of nine blocks. This bottom row is the same inventory bar that is seen under my health and hunger meters when my inventory is closed, on the main game screen. These are items I can access without having to press E, either by selecting them with the mouse or by using the number keys, each assigned to one inventory slot from 1 to 9.

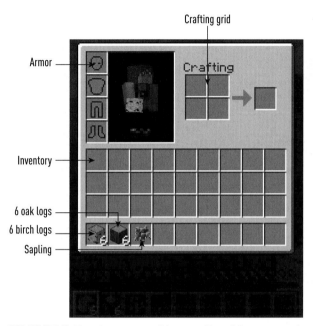

FIGURE 5.5 Your inventory, with a small crafting space, slots for armor, and slots for up to 36 different items

There are a couple of steps to making a crafting bench. First, I need to convert some of the logs into wood planks. Since one log makes four planks and a crafting bench is made from four planks, I need some more planks to make tools. I will convert two logs to create eight planks.

This is done by dragging and dropping logs into the 4 × 4 crafting space in the upper-right corner of the inventory screen (**Figure 5.6**). When blocks are placed in the right order and location in a crafting grid, the crafted object appears automatically in the box to the right of the grid. This is also true of items crafted on a full-size crafting bench. There are dozens of crafted items that can be made, and the placement of the base materials is known as a *recipe*. Recipes are constantly changing as new materials are added by Mojang, so the best place to find current recipes, or crafting plans, is the Minecraft wiki.

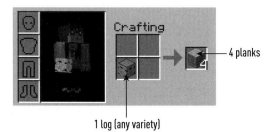

1 log (any variety)

FIGURE 5.6 Crafting wood planks from logs

Once I have four planks, I can pick them up and drop them into my inventory or back into the crafting grid as needed. When I place one in each square of the crafting grid, it makes a crafting bench automatically (**Figure 5.7**).

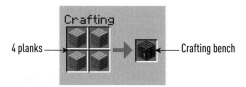

FIGURE 5.7 Making a crafting bench

I can carry the crafting bench in my inventory, but will not be able to use it until I place it on the ground (**Figure 5.8**).

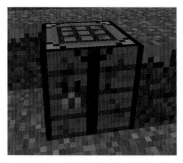

FIGURE 5.8 A crafting bench is the first and most important tool to make as you start the game, because very little can be made without it.

STEP 3: MAKE A PICK

To mine for ore materials, it helps to have a pickaxe. Although some ores, such as stone, can be punched in the same manner as trees, it takes considerable time to produce results. Iron ores must be mined with at least a stone pick; wooden picks won't do the job. Ores such as diamond, gold, and emerald require an iron pick. There is a progression here, so the goals must be met in order to move to the next step.

I'll start by making a simple wooden pick. I click my placed crafting bench, and a 9 x 9 crafting grid appears, along with a view of my inventory to make crafting simpler. I place two blocks of wood, one above the other, in the crafting table to make wooden sticks. This is a simple recipe that never changes. Sticks can be used as handles for tools, combined with charcoal or coal to make torches, and used in other crafted items, such as fences and gates (**Figure 5.9**).

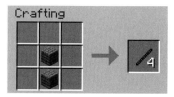

FIGURE 5.9 Crafting sticks to make a handle for a pick

I can combine two wooden sticks with three wooden planks to make a pickaxe. This pick will last for just a little while, as all tools suffer from wear. I've used all my planks to make the crafting table and these sticks, so I will need to convert another log into planks before I can proceed.

The recipe for making a pick will never change, though the materials will, depending on whether you want to make a stone, iron, or diamond pick. In those cases, I would replace the top row of planks with the materials of my choice (**Figure 5.10**).

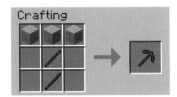

FIGURE 5.10 Crafting a wooden pickaxe

STEP 4: MINE FOR ORES AND MAKE A SHELTER

I need to mine stone to make a furnace for cooking and to make stone tools for mining ores. Since there is a small hill of exposed rock at the spawn point, I'm going to make my home for the night right in the hill. I can mine for the ores I need and also create a cave for shelter before the sun goes down and the hostile mobs come out to play.

I use my wooden pick to dig into the hill. To do this, I equip the pick by scrolling the mouse pointer over it on the inventory bar; the pick appears in my hand. I use the left mouse button to dig at the materials directly in front of me, and soon I've dug out enough dirt and stone to make a rough cave. The dirt and stone I dig up end up in inventory as well.

STEP 5: MAKE STONE TOOLS

Now that I have my shelter and some stone, I am going to make a furnace, a stone pick, and a stone sword. I'll need a sword (**Figure 5.11**) to collect chicken for my dinner and defend myself from mobs, so I use the crafting table to make one—again, by dragging the materials from my inventory into the pattern that will make a sword.

Since I still have plenty of stone, I will make a stone pick, with three blocks of stone where the wooden planks were. This pick allows me to mine for ores such as iron, and it's also more efficient and longer-lasting than a wooden pick for mining stone.

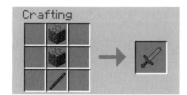

FIGURE 5.11 A simple stone sword

Finally, a furnace (**Figure 5.12**) made of eight stones will allow me to cook meat and smelt ores such as iron and gold. I need wood or coal for fuel, but since I already have a good amount of wood, I won't bother looking for coal just yet (although it is a more efficient fuel).

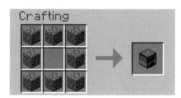

FIGURE 5.12 Crafting a furnace, an oft-used tool for cooking meat and smelting ore

I've used my stone pick to move my crafting bench from outside to inside the cave with my furnace so I can work during the night when I'm hiding from mobs (**Figure 5.13**).

FIGURE 5.13 My dark and simple abode for the first night. Nothing fancy, but the tools I need are there!

NOTE See how my inventory shows my sword, pick, trees, and more?

STEP 6: GET FOOD

I'm heading out because there is food nearby in the form of those chickens. I want to be back at my den before nightfall, but returning with chicken isn't a bad thing at all.

Chickens (**Figure 5.14**) lay eggs, which are used in some recipes. When they die, they drop raw meat and sometimes feathers.

FIGURE 5.14 Dinner: a chicken, with a bonus egg

STEP 7: SHELTER FOR THE NIGHT

Assessing my inventory (**Figure 5.15**), I have quite a few items now, from tools to items dropped by the chickens to ores and dirt.

Having found nine chickens, I head back to my cave as the sun begins to go down. I am going to simply wall myself in, but it will be dark, so I'm going to make a light.

FIGURE 5.15 My updated inventory: raw chicken, feathers, and eggs from my hunting; the tools I crafted; some stone and wood; and some seeds I picked up.

If I'd been able to find coal ore, I would have used that to craft torches, but since I didn't, I'll make some charcoal by burning logs in my furnace. I'll combine the charcoal with sticks to make torches (**Figure 5.16**).

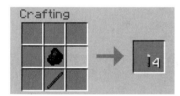

FIGURE 5.16 Torches, a much needed source of light

Now that I have shelter, light, and fuel, I'll cook up those chickens in the furnace. I drag the raw chicken into the top box and my fuel into the bottom (**Figure 5.17**). As soon as both boxes are filled with the correct items, the furnace will begin to cook the chicken, and I can leave it in the furnace if I have other things to do.

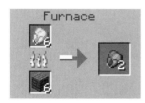

FIGURE 5.17 Making roast chicken for dinner

STEP 8: A BRAND NEW DAY

After about eight minutes, the length of a night, I can head outside for a day of exploring and adventure, having successfully survived the night!

> **NOTE** In Minecraft, a day is 12 minutes and a night is 8 minutes, giving us a consistent 20-minute day/night cycle.

MY CONFESSION

OK, two confessions, one of which will come as no surprise to anyone who knows my gaming skills.

The first is that although I have enthusiasm, I am not the best of players. I mess up. A lot. Often with hilarious results, though I may not see the humor as much as my fellow players do. That being said, I have no problem poking fun at myself.

This first confession leads me to my second: I cheated in writing this chapter.

I completely and absolutely failed to make it through the first night. Not only that, but I died repeatedly. It became farcical and awesome, to be honest, because of the many and varied ways I died. Wrednax didn't help matters, because he was giving a play-by-play to one of our Rawcritics friends the entire time. We were both laughing so hard—another factor in my inability to stay alive.

I lost track of time. Suddenly it was dark and the mobs were on the move. My first death was from a simple zombie attack as I was making a stone sword—I was dead before I realized what had happened.

My spawn point was about 25 blocks away, through some water. I managed to make it back to the cave and was trying to wall myself in when the baby zombie struck. Baby zombies are much, much faster and fiercer than most of the mobs, and tougher to kill. Death two.

Endermen are tall creatures with glowing eyes—if you avoid eye contact, they ignore you. If you're eye to eye with one, like I was the moment I spawned, they are swift and merciless. Death three.

Death four was another baby zombie, who was already around a corner in my cave when I got there. I should have known.

Death five? That same enderman. Again. Couldn't be avoided.

One last try. I approached my den, only to be chased by two zombies carrying wood blocks that I had lost when they'd killed me before. Insult to injury. I turned around to make my escape and landed right in the arms of a green creeper. Creepers are of course anything but friendly. Cue the massive explosion and subsequent death.

By now Wrednax and I were laughing so hard we were crying. Wrednax was busy giving our friend jsfm a running commentary, and we knew there was no way I'd make it through the first night in my cave. I went the opposite direction, to the sandy beach.

Sand is very easy to dig with your bare hands, but you suffocate if you're buried in it. I dug one dirt block as I passed, then I reached the beach and dug down. And then I placed the dirt block over my head and waited for sunrise.

Which, really, is a completely valid and viable alternative way to stay alive!

CHAPTER 6

BASIC GAMEPLAY

IN CHAPTER 5, we walked through a first night. We looked at how to start a new game and some gameplay basics—using a crafting bench and furnace and crafting and using basic tools. All this activity was in the framework of actually playing the game. In this chapter, we'll look at Minecraft basics in a bit more depth.

There is far more to Minecraft than we can cover in this book, and with regular game updates that introduce items, blocks, mobs, and more, keeping current is a tricky proposition. Encourage your kids to explore and discover as much as they can about the game themselves. And if you can do the same alongside them, so much the better. You'll be learning together and helping each other make discoveries.

Bookmark the site http://minecraft.gamepedia.com/Minecraft_Wiki. This wiki site contains all things Minecraft and is constantly updated by players. Every mob and every item has its own page, along with building ideas, detailed information on mining and farm plans, and in-depth technical information such as game algorithms. Anything you can think of, you'll find on the wiki pages. There is a search box, and it is easy to navigate. I'll be giving you the basics, but for more information on the topics throughout this chapter, refer to the wiki.

For any other questions, online searches are your best bet. You'll want to be aware of your game version, and check that you're looking at tutorials and answers that are as up to date as possible.

Now let's get into the fun part: the game itself.

STARTING A NEW GAME

The new game we created in Chapter 5 was in Survival mode, using just the basic settings. Let's look at a few more options you can explore in Survival mode.

1. Open Minecraft by double-clicking the Minecraft launcher icon, and log in with your email address and password.

NOTE   Once you log in to Minecraft, you'll remain logged in, even if you close your browser, unless you click Log Out under your username on the log in page.

2. Click the Play button at the bottom to go to the main Minecraft window.

3. Click the Singleplayer button. You'll be taken to the Select World window.

4. Click the Create New World button to start a new world.

This takes you to the Create New World window (**Figure 6.1**).

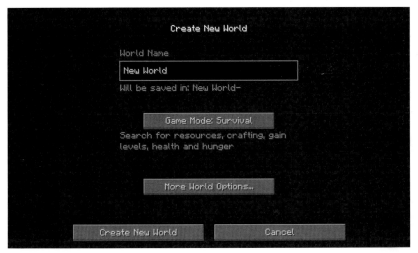

FIGURE 6.1 In the Create New World window, you can name your world, select a game mode, and use the More World Options button to customize your environment.

5. Enter a name for this world in the World Name field, and keep the game mode set to the default, Survival.

6. Click More World Options to be taken to a new window with more options to further customize your world (**Figure 6.2**).

7. Once you have made your selections, click the Create New World button. You can also click Done and be returned to the Create New World page. Remember that when you have created your world, you will not be able to go back and change these settings.

> **NOTE** The Allow Cheats and Bonus Chest buttons are available when you create a Survival or Creative world but not a Hardcore world.

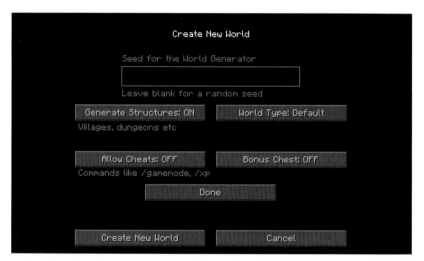

FIGURE 6.2 The World Options window allows you to customize your world before you generate it.

WORLD SEEDS

World seeds are a fun way to explore and experiment with worlds. Every time you start a new game, a new world is formed for you. Each world has a unique code called a *world seed* that you can enter in the Seed For World Generator field in the Create New World window (Figure 6.2) to replicate a world type you've created or found online. If you leave this field blank when you create a new world, Minecraft will create a world from a random seed.

To find the seed of the game you are playing, type **/** to open the command bar, type **seed**, and then press Enter. The seed name will appear in the command bar. If you want to generate a world using this seed, enter it in the Seed For The World Generator field when you create a new world.

An online search for "Minecraft world seeds" will result in pages on which people have posted seeds they found particularly useful or fun, usually with a description and often with pictures.

GENERATE STRUCTURES

Structures in Minecraft include villages, abandoned mineshafts, dungeons, and strongholds. Clicking the Generate Structures button toggles structures on and off.

- Villages are populated with villagers who will trade items with you and who have buildings, gardens, and often a chest with useful items.

- Abandoned mineshafts are below ground and also have chests, although they also often have dungeons with monster spawners and more chests.

- Dungeons appear in caves underground.

- Strongholds are rare and are filled with chests with less common treasures, as well as a portal to the End, which we will look at later in this chapter.

When you begin playing, it is helpful to have Generate Structures turned on. Villager trading is helpful, and finding chests in structures can be both exciting and very useful to gameplay.

WORLD TYPE

The World Type button allows you to cycle through and select the type of world that will be generated. Worlds are created from a variety of biomes, or ecosystems, and offer different climates, plants, animals, and geographic features such as swamps, mountains, and plains.

The Default setting is for regular-size biomes, which you can traverse in a fairly short walk so that you can go from swamp to jungle quickly, for example. This is handy if you're collecting resources specific to different biomes.

The Superflat setting is just as it sounds. This world type has no biomes, and is just a few layers of dirt over bedrock, and therefore works well for Creative mode. The flat landscape that goes on for thousands of blocks is perfect for experimenting with buildings and landforms. If you select Superflat, you'll get a Customize option for setting what the layers of ground consist of, such as dirt or water. Other preset options include desert and water worlds.

The Large Biome setting generates a world four times larger than the Default biome. If you are planning a large build, perhaps an Egyptian-themed city in a desert, you might want to switch to large biomes to ensure that you have the space you need without having to resort to extreme terraforming by hand.

ALLOW CHEATS

Minecraft gives you the option of turning on *cheats* for gameplay. Cheats are commands you can type in the command bar (accessed by pressing **/**. Once you press **/**, you can press the Tab key to see the available cheats, such as */tp* to teleport and */weather* to change the weather). The single-player survival game doesn't offer really useful cheats—such as Fly or God mode—so it may not be of much use to have them on, but it can be fun to experiment.

BONUS CHEST

When you have Bonus Chest enabled, your game will generate with a bonus chest at your spawn point (**Figure 6.3**). This chest will have some basic random materials to get you started, such as wood, wooden tools, and food. This is a good option to turn on, particularly for new players.

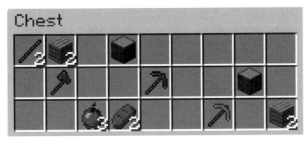

FIGURE 6.3 A sample of the contents of a bonus chest at spawn.

BASIC COMMANDS

My biggest challenge when I began to play Minecraft was just moving around. Although I'd played games on the computer long ago, in recent years I'd become strictly a console gamer, which means I played on consoles hooked up to my TV, such as the Nintendo systems. Switching to the keyboard was a challenge. Thankfully, it didn't take too long for me to get used to moving around, and it won't for you either, although you'll likely be jealous of how easy your kids make it look long before you get the hang of it!

■ KEYBOARD AND MOUSE COMMANDS

In Minecraft, you use your keyboard and mouse for everything. Pressing the W, A, S, or D key moves you forward, left, back, and right, respectively. Pressing E displays your inventory, the spacebar lets you jump, and Shift lets you crouch. And as if those weren't confusing enough, you use your left and right mouse keys to dig and place blocks and to attack. These are standard for most computer games, but if you're new to using a keyboard to play games, trying to remember them can be frustrating, especially when you're facing mobs.

Thankfully, you can access a list of the commands by pressing the Esc key to open the game menu, and then clicking Options. In the

Options window, click the Controls button to see which keys and clicks do what (you can also reassign keys and mouse clicks, if, for example, you are left-handed and want to shift keyboarding responsibilities to your right hand). **Table 6.1** lists the keyboard and mouse commands. Get to know these commands; the best way to learn them is by playing.

TABLE 6.1 Keyboard and Mouse Commands

Key	Action
W	Go forward (double tap and hold to sprint).
S	Go back.
A	Go left.
D	Go right.
Spacebar	Jump. Creative mode only: Double tapping allows you to fly.
Left Shift	Crouch and sneak. Sneaking means that other players will not be able to see your name displayed above your player's head. Creative mode only: Use to descend when flying.
E	Open inventory.
Q	Drop whatever you are holding.
T	Opens the command bar, used to chat in multiplayer games.
Left-click	Break blocks. Use tools to dig and sword to attack. Pick up and move items in inventory and chests.
Right-click	Place blocks. Block with your sword; draw your bow. Eat, and drink potions. Open chests; push buttons and levers. Use tools like shears, fishing rod, and leads.
F1	Turn the onscreen display on and off.
F2	Take a screenshot.

Key	Action
F3	Shows game information, such as your coordinates and game speed in fps (frames per second).
F5	Cycle through first-, second-, and third-person point of view.
Tab	List current players.

◼ NAVIGATING YOUR INVENTORY

In Chapter 5, we looked at the health and food meters on your main game screen, as well as your inventory. The nine inventory boxes on your main screen are also known as your *hotkey slots*. To access the items in this inventory bar, move your cursor over them, or use what are known as *hotkeys*—the numbers 1 though 9 on your keyboard, which correspond to the slots in your inventory. This is a quick way to access your items, although it isn't always intuitive when you start playing.

When you press E, you open your inventory. You can left-click to pick up and place items around your inventory, or between your inventory and a chest. If you left-click to pick up a stack of items and continue holding the button down as you drag your mouse cursor across your inventory, crafting bench, or furnace, you'll drop equal numbers of blocks into each square you pass over. This is really helpful for crafting items. A right-click will pick up half of whatever stack of items you are on. This is useful when you are dividing items into two parts.

◼ CREATIVE WORLDS

A world set to Creative mode offers a couple of differences in game commands than worlds set to other modes. Creative also offers a new movement—flight—and its inventory management is different too.

MOVEMENT COMMANDS

In Creative worlds, you have access to all the movement commands; however, you can also fly, which is a huge bonus when you are working on tall builds or wanting to view something from above.

To fly, double-click the spacebar. Holding the spacebar makes you gain altitude. Tapping it again will turn off flight and you'll fall, but don't worry, you can't die on Creative. And if you're fast, you can reactivate flight by double-tapping the spacebar again. You still navigate using the W, A, S, and D keys—to fly and go forward, press W+spacebar.

Pressing the left Shift key will allow you to descend. If, once you're in the air, you double-tap the left Shift key, nothing will happen, unlike the spacebar toggling flight on and off.

INVENTORY

The other major difference between Survival and Creative is how your inventory functions. On Creative, when you access your inventory with the E key, you get a multi-tabbed, full inventory, offering access to every single block and item. In Creative, you get to create without having to find your materials (**Figure 6.4**).

Items in your inventory are divided into categories, including Building and Decoration Blocks, Tools, and Combat. You can move from tab to tab and add items to your hotkeys slots. To remove items from your hotkey slots, just drag them with your mouse over the main inventory and drop them. It doesn't need to be over the same item, or even in the same category. Your inventory also comes with a search function, denoted by a compass in the upper-right corner. There is a chest for a survival-style inventory, where you can also equip armor, in the lower-right corner.

FIGURE 6.4 Your inventory on Creative is different than on Survival, with complete access to all blocks and items in the game, including one or two not found in Survival.

BIOMES AND TERRAIN

Much like the real world, Minecraft has biomes, specific areas of terrain that have unique properties such as plants and weather systems (**Figure 6.5**). These biomes are randomly created when a new world is generated. On the Default map (as opposed to one where Large Biomes was selected under World Type), you can usually travel from one biome to another fairly rapidly. This is helpful because certain materials are easier to find in specific biomes, such as sand in a desert or beach. Other materials can be found only in a specific biome, such as jungle wood and cocoa beans in a jungle.

FIGURE 6.5 Some of the biomes you'll find in Minecraft. Top: Jungle, Taiga, Extreme Hills; Middle: the Nether, Forest, the End; Bottom: Desert (with jungle behind), Swamp.

Exploring biomes can be fun. Here's a brief summary of some of the main biomes. Go for a walkabout, or send your child on one, and see what each has to offer. For more information, see the biomes page at the Minecraft wiki (http://minecraft.gamepedia.com/biomes).

PLAINS

- Grassy flatlands.

- Home to horses, cows, sheep, and pigs.

- NPC (non-player character) villages are found here.

FOREST

- Oak and birch woodlands, not overly dense.

SWAMP

- Wetlands, often found along shorelines.

- Home to witches and slimes.

- Good source of sand, clay, and reeds.

JUNGLE

- Thick forests with tall jungle wood trees (which produce cocoa beans) and vines.

- Jungle temples can be found here.

- Only place to find ocelots.

DESERT

- Cactus-dotted sand and sandstone terrain.

- Desert temples and NPC villages appear here.

TAIGA

- Much like a forest, but filled with snow-covered spruce trees and frozen ponds and rivers.

- Wolves are found here.

EXTREME HILLS

- High and steep hills, mountains, and cliffs.

- Only place to find emeralds.

MUSHROOM ISLAND

- Rare biome.

- Rare giant mushrooms grow here, and mycelium blocks and mooshrooms (mushroom-covered red cows) are found only in this biome.

HELL/NETHER

- Biome accessed only through a Nether portal. It has its own map and is all underground.

- Blocks include netherrack, quartz, glowstone, and soul sand, all of which can be found only in the Nether.

- Water evaporates here, so all seas and rivers are formed of lava.

- Mobs unique to the Nether include magma cubes, ghasts, blazes, wither skeletons, and zombie pigmen.

- Nether fortresses are found only in the Nether.

NETHER PORTAL

A Nether portal is required to enter the Nether. The wiki covers the Nether and Nether portals in great detail and offers useful ways to make shortcuts through the overworld by using Nether portals.

To make a Nether portal, you need to make a frame out of obsidian (a hard stone created from lava and water; it requires a diamond pick to mine); the corners can be any material. It needs to be four blocks wide and five blocks high. Once you have a frame, light the inside on fire with lava, flint, and steel or by using a fire charge. The center will fill with swirling purple light. Step into the opening to be transported to the Nether (**Figure 6.6**).

Placement of a Nether portal in the overworld and its corresponding location in the Nether can be confusing if you are trying to use portals to travel across a map. It's helpful to know that traveling one block in the Nether is the same as traveling eight blocks on the main map.

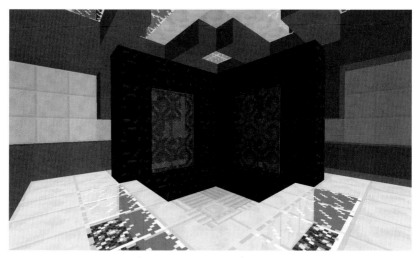

FIGURE 6.6 A Nether portal (two are shown here) will take you to the Nether.

SKY/END

- A separate biome accessed only through an End portal, which can be found only in a stronghold.

- Made of End stone and populated by endermen and the ender dragon.

END PORTAL

To find an End portal, you must first find a stronghold, which are rare and spawn underground. Inside the fortress, you'll find an End portal, which you must activate. You need to use Eyes of Ender to first locate the stronghold and then to activate the End portal (**Figure 6.7**).

FIGURE 6.7 An Eye of Ender, used to find strongholds and activate the End portal.

Other biomes include oceans and ice plains. At the time of this writing, update 1.7 is in the works and will bring new biomes, including Savannah and Mesa. Go exploring—it's fun!

MOBS

Many creatures populate the Minecraft world, from farm animals such as pigs and cows to monsters like zombies and skeletons. In Minecraft, these are known as *mobs*, a long-standing video game term short for *mobile,* as they are mobile entities that can move around the game.

Mobs appear, or spawn, throughout the game world, although some are designed to appear only in specific areas or biomes (squid spawn only in water, for example). Some mobs are considered friendly and passive, such as livestock, and are sometimes called *critters*. Other mobs are aggressive and known as *monsters* or *hostile mobs*. A few mobs, such as wolves and zombie pigmen, are in a different category—they are neutral unless you attack them first. You can coexist alongside this last group without fear of attack; in the case of wolves, you can even tame them to create a domesticated dog. Should you hit one, however, even accidentally, their attack will be swift.

The game includes a couple of other types of mobs. A villager is also known as an NPC (non-player character). Villagers spawn in villages and do not drop items upon death (more on this in the next section), but they do have a trade function—you can trade items for other, sometimes rare, items. Zombies are attracted to villagers and will try to attack them, so villagers automatically enter their houses at night to avoid zombie sieges. A villager attacked by a zombie becomes a zombie villager and is a hostile mob.

You can create golems, both iron and snow, which can be used to protect players; iron golems can be used to protect villagers. Iron golems can also spawn in villages if the conditions are right.

Domestic animals can spawn at any time, but monsters spawn only in places with low light—at night, in caves or mineshafts, and in other shaded areas. Creating lit areas, such as with torches, can help prevent mobs from spawning. When daylight comes, most hostile mobs will catch fire and burn up, dropping items when they do. While they are on fire, they are still hostile and will attack. If players approach too closely, they too can catch fire, so take care when gathering items.

 NOTE If you are interested in a more in-depth look at each mob, go to the Minecraft wiki.

◼ KILLING MOBS AND MOB DROPS

All mobs can be killed, some with a little more difficulty than others. Using a bow and arrow or sword are the most efficient methods, and using enchanted weapons is even more effective. Most mobs, when killed, will drop at least one and sometimes two useful items, which are known as *mob drops*. If you use a sword with a looting enchantment, your chances of getting more of each item rise. Upon death, mobs also release experience points for players, in the form of glowing green balls. Mob deaths can be distressing for some players, because needed items, such as leather from cows (which also drop beef), can be acquired only by killing a mob, often a friendly one. In Minecraft there is no blood or gore, but it still requires you to hit the critter or monster until they die and drop an item. When hit, mobs flash a reddish hue and bounce back a little ways. Some families (particularly those with younger or more sensitive children) prefer to play solely on Creative worlds because in Creative mode every possible item is freely available without having to kill mobs.

BREEDING AND TAMING MOBS

You can breed many of the friendly mobs by feeding two of them specific items such as wheat or seeds. The two animals will touch each other, and when they part there will be a baby between them; the player gets experience points. This is a good way to raise animals to farm. Wolves and ocelots can also be fed, which will turn them into pet dogs and cats and bond them to the player who tamed them. Horses can be trained and ridden but will not attach to a specific player.

Let's take a look at some mobs, including what they drop, how to breed them, and how to kill them. The "Drops" sections list all the items it is possible for a mob to drop, but a mob will not typically drop more than two items from the list, unless you have a looting sword.

FRIENDLY MOBS

You can find many friendly mobs scattered across the map. These are great for farming. If you build pens or barns, you can lead a pair of animals with food (usually wheat, though chickens follow seeds) or by making a lead out of string and a slime ball. Once you have a pair of animals, you can breed them for an endless supply of food and mob drops.

If you have an older computer, large farms may cause it to slow down or lag. You might need to decrease the size of your farm or spread it out over more space to improve your computer's performance.

COWS

Drops: Leather; raw beef; milk when touched with an empty bucket (milking does not kill the cow).

Cows spawn in grassy areas and are extremely useful. Use their leather for making armor, books, and item frames and their beef for food.

Cows can be bred using wheat, and they make excellent farm animals.

MOOSHROOMS

Drops: Leather; raw beef; milk when touched with an empty bucket (does not kill the mooshroom); mushroom stew when tapped with a wooden bowl (does not kill the mooshroom); mushrooms when sheared, though this turns them into a cow.

Mooshrooms are perhaps the cutest mob in Minecraft and the most versatile. A mooshroom will give an endless supply of stew, as well as the drops that cows provide.

Mooshrooms are rare. They spawn only on the Mooshroom Island biome, which often takes quite a bit of exploring to find.

Like cows, mooshrooms can be bred with wheat and are useful farm animals.

SHEEP

Drops: Wool, though it's more efficient to shear sheep with shears rather than kill them.

Sheep are useful as a source of wool for building and decorating (both as wool blocks and crafted to make carpets) rather than as a food source. Wool is also needed to make a bed.

Sheep spawn in grassy areas.

When sheep are sheared, they will drop one to three blocks of wool, which will grow back when they eat grass. The wool can be dyed one of 16 colors. Sheep spawn in white, brown, black, gray, light gray, and occasionally pink, but they can be dyed any color by clicking them with a dye (the dye is then used up). You can dye individual blocks of wool, but each uses one dye, whereas if you dye the sheep itself, you can shear it and the wool will grow back the same color as the dye, making them a great renewable resource. Sheep can also be redyed other colors.

Breed sheep with wheat. When two sheep of different colors are bred, the offspring typically will be one of the two colors, though occasionally they are a blend of the two colors.

PIGS

Drops: Raw pork.

Pigs are a source of pork but otherwise don't provide any real benefits. They spawn in grassy areas and can be bred with wheat.

Ride pigs by placing a saddle on them and then guide them with a carrot on a stick, which is crafted by putting a carrot on a fishing rod in a crafting table.

Occasionally, pigs can be hit by lightning, turning them into zombie pigmen.

CHICKENS

Drops: Raw chicken and feathers when killed; eggs.

Chickens make good farm animals; they lay seven eggs as they wander around, and they drop raw chicken when they are killed. They also drop feathers, which are needed to make arrows and quill pens.

You can sometimes hatch chicks by throwing eggs, and they can be bred with seeds.

HORSES, DONKEYS, AND MULES

Drops: Leather, though horses are not typically bred for drops.

Horses, donkeys, and mules (which I'll hereafter lump together as horses unless specified) spawn only in plains. Horses can be ridden, and donkeys and mules can carry a chest. There are also horse monsters, in the form of zombie and skeleton horses.

Different horses travel at different speeds and can jump in varying heights. Riding even the slowest horse is faster than traveling on foot, and most horses travel at impressive speeds.

You tame a horse by riding it (right-click to mount; left-Shift to dismount); expect to be thrown several times. When the horse calms and is marked with floating hearts, you have succeeded in taming it. Once it is tamed, you can breed and ride the horse.

To ride horses (if you want to control them), you need a saddle, currently found only in dungeons, temples, and blacksmith chests or by trading with villagers. It is impossible to create on your own. You can find horse armor in various dungeon chests.

Horses are bred with golden carrots and apples, which are crafted by surrounding the carrots or apples with eight gold ingots. You can breed two horses, two donkeys, or a horse and a donkey (which will produce a mule). As in real life, mules are sterile. Horses come in several colors and can have one of five types of markings, which means there are 35 different appearances, by far the greatest variety of all the mobs in the game.

Horses can be fed a variety of food, including sugar, apples, carrots, bread, wheat, and hay, and the various foods have different effects. They are unique among mobs in that they have their own health meters and a special inventory for their armor.

SQUID

Drops: Ink sacs, used for making dye and for writing in books.

Squid spawn in bodies of water. They cannot be bred, and really are only useful for their ink sac drops.

OCELOTS/CATS

Drops: None.

Ocelots are wild cats that appear in jungles. They are shy and will run away from you. With patience and a good supply of raw fish, you can tame them and they will turn into cats (Siamese, tabby, or black-and-white tuxedo). Taming cats requires some perseverance, because the ocelots are shy and must approach you. Crouching (using the left-Shift key) while holding a fish is a good way to attract them, as is walking toward them slowly. Chasing ocelots will make them run away. When the ocelot looks at you, stay still, don't look directly at it, and wait for it to approach you. Right-click it with the fish, carefully. If it senses movement, it will run away. This can take up to 20 fish, but be patient. Once tamed, it will become a cat.

Cats will follow you, so they can end up in danger from things such as lava, fire, and cactus. Because they become pets, it can be more distressing if they die, so if you're going somewhere that they might be in danger, make them sit by right-clicking them. If they are not seated, they will teleport to you.

Cats like to sit on beds, chests, and furnaces, which make them a bit of a nuisance, but they won't sit on anything with a block directly above it. Cats and especially kittens will run through your crops. Use raw fish to breed kittens, which will have the same coloring as whichever cat you fed fish to first.

Creepers avoid cats. Cats can see players who are using an invisibility potion and will often watch them.

BATS

Drops: None.

Bats are cute cave-dwelling critters, but that's about it. They don't attack, nor do they drop anything when killed.

VILLAGERS

Drops: None.

NPC villagers (sometimes called *testificates*) are passive mobs that you can interact with. They are found only in villages. Villagers wear various-colored robes that mark their occupations, such as butchers and farmers, and each trades different items, such as fish for an emerald, or a piece of armor for coal. Each starts out with one item they will trade, and every time you make a trade, a new item is added to the options. Some trades are not equal or fair, but to open up a variety of trade options you might need to make the exchange they are requesting.

Villagers breed on their own, so long as they have enough buildings with doors. The game uses a specific formula for this that includes rules about door number and placement. Villagers are also vulnerable to zombies, and will become zombie villagers if they are attacked. For this reason, when night falls, they will enter their village houses on their own—another reason why buildings with doors are so important.

■ NEUTRAL MOBS

These mobs are neutral, meaning they will leave you alone... so long as you leave them alone. Hitting one—or, in the case of endermen, looking one in the eye—will bring on fierce retaliation.

WOLVES/DOGS

Drops: None.

Wolves are neutral mobs that can become hostile when attacked. You'll find them mostly in Taiga biomes (snowy forest) and occasionally in forests; wolves tend to run in packs. You can tame one by feeding it bones until it displays hearts and a collar appears around its neck (collars are red, but can be dyed by right-clicking with dye in your hand). Tamed wolves are known as dogs, and they will follow you and protect you from hostile mobs or other players. They will also teleport to you, much like cats do. Right-clicking them makes them sit and stay, which is handy if you are going somewhere where they might be in the way or in danger, like where there is a lot of lava.

You can breed dogs by feeding them any meat, and the puppies will also be tame.

If you should hit a wolf, even accidentally, it will become a hostile mob with red eyes and will attack any player in the area. Wolves also become hostile around sheep and will kill a flock, though they revert back to neutral in this situation.

ENDERMEN

Drops: Ender pearls. If you throw ender pearls, you are instantly teleported to their landing spot; ender pearls are necessary for crafting an Eye of Ender (which is needed to create and activate an End portal).

Endermen are from the End, but will spawn throughout the game. They take damage from water, but unlike most of the hostile mobs, they can exist in sunlight. You are safe from endermen so long as you don't look at their faces—this means keeping your onscreen crosshairs on their legs.

If you take a pumpkin and wear it like a helmet (placing a pumpkin in your inventory where your helmet would go allows you to wear it), you'll be immune to the enderman's stare, but pumpkin helmets obstruct your vision.

Endermen can teleport, and if you happen to look at one, even from a great distance, you might find that it has appeared directly behind you and is on the attack. They are incredibly powerful, so you might be killed before you even realize you're under attack.

While endermen in general are peaceful (unless you look at them), they can be frustrating, because they can pick up and move blocks. They don't restrict themselves to dirt and stone, but they might remove blocks from your home or farm.

ZOMBIE PIGMEN

Drops: Rotten flesh, golden ingots, golden bars, and golden swords.

Zombie pigmen live in the Nether, although they occasionally come through Nether portals. They can be created when lightning strikes a pig, though this is rare.

Zombie pigmen are peaceful unless they are hit, even accidentally—then they will go on the attack and all zombie pigmen in the area will join in. They are fierce and won't stop even after you die. If you return to collect your belongings, they will continue attacking until they all die. This can be incredibly frustrating, particularly if they are blocking your access to the Nether or you are trying to reclaim lost items. With preparation, it is not too difficult to kill zombie pigmen if you can get them one at a time.

■ HOSTILE MOBS

Hostile mobs, or monsters, are out to get you. They spawn at night or in low light, and most ignite in the daylight. Their drops can be useful—skeleton bones can be turned into bonemeal, which helps plants grow, and spider string is needed to craft fishing rods and bows.

ZOMBIES, BABY ZOMBIES, AND ZOMBIE VILLAGERS

Drops: Raw flesh, and occasionally carrots, potatos, iron bars, a piece of armor, shovels, or swords.

Zombies are a common hostile mob that spawns at night or in dark places. They are slow-moving and can be fairly easy to kill if you are prepared, but if you don't have a good weapon or armor, they can kill you just as easily. An injured zombie attacks with more force, and more zombies can spawn in the area of the one you are attacking.

Zombies burst into flame at daylight but will still attack; if they come close to you, you'll catch on fire as well.

Zombies can wear armor, including armor with minor enchantments, and occasionally will attack with a shovel or sword. Sometimes they drop their armor or weapons on death. If you die, they may equip themselves with some of the items you dropped, adding insult to injury.

Baby zombies are similar to adults, but much more terrifying. They are faster and can fit into one-block openings. They can appear in daylight.

Zombie villagers act in the same manner as zombies but look like zombified villagers. They are villagers that a zombie has attacked. They can be turned back into villagers through a somewhat lengthy process—once you have potion-making abilities and materials.

SKELETONS

Drops: Bones, arrows, a bow, and armor.

Skeletons, like zombies, spawn in the dark and burn in daylight. They are armed with bows and can attack from a distance. Like zombies, they can pick up dropped items and use them, including armor.

Skeletons shoot arrows faster the closer you are, so it is a good idea to practice using a bow yourself so you can deal with them at a distance. It is possible to kill them with a sword; wearing armor will help you live long enough to get within arm's reach.

SPIDERS, CAVE SPIDERS, AND SPIDER JOCKEYS

Drops: Strings and spider eyes.

Spiders, like zombies and skeletons, attack at night. They won't always disappear during the day, but they won't attack either.

Spiders drop strings and spider eyes, which are useful for potions. They are faster than the other mobs and can jump and climb, albeit clumsily. Being long and low, they can fit into a one-block-high space as long as it is two blocks wide.

Cave spiders are venomous. They are also much smaller and can fit through small spaces with ease, making them doubly dangerous. If you are bitten by a cave spider, your hearts will turn a pale green and start to decrease until the venom wears off or you die. Drinking milk can stop the poison, but the spiders will continue to bite and you'll be reinfected, so killing them quickly is your best course of action. They emerge only from spawners (blocks that resemble cages and discharge monsters) in dungeons and abandoned mineshafts. Because bright light stops them from spawning, lighting the spawner and area around it as fast as possible is a good tactic, as is pouring lava in the space (but be careful you don't get burned!).

Spider jockeys are rare. These are spiders with skeletons riding them, so you need to not only worry about a speedier foe but also watch out for arrows. If you don't have good armor or weapons, particularly a bow, it's best to make a speedy escape. Even if you kill one of the pair, the other will keep after you.

CREEPERS

Drops: Gunpowder; if killed by a skeleton, a music disc.

These green, hissing mobs have become an icon of Minecraft. Creepers attack by approaching and then exploding, taking out a portion of the area around them at the same time. This can be extremely frustrating if they destroy part of a build. They alert you to their presence with a hissing sound, but this is not long before they explode, so you need to react quickly.

Creepers spawn at night and in low-light areas but don't catch fire during the day. They can be fought back in close combat if you keep a few blocks between you and them. It is possible to lure them away from builds, as they will follow players.

SLIMES

Drops: Slime balls.

Slimes spawn in swamps at night and very occasionally in deep caves. These large green bouncing cubes are tricky in that they divide as you attack them, so that one large slime breaks into two smaller ones, which form two smaller ones, and so on, and each of them needs to be dealt with. The smallest don't cause damage, and since the big ones need to be in contact with you to hurt you, if you're nimble you can deal with them fairly easily.

Each small slime drops a slime ball, which is used in leads, in fire charges for fireworks, and in creating sticky pistons.

SILVERFISH

Drops: None.

Silverfish are small bugs that hide in strongholds and occasionally in the Extreme Hills biome. They hide in blocks that look like regular blocks, but when they are mined, a silverfish will come out. If a silverfish is attacked, it will call other silverfish to its aid. If enough appear, they can do a lot of damage to the player and to the area, breaking blocks as they move about. You must take care dealing with them. Lava works well for killing silverfish.

WITCHES

Drops: Bottles, glowstone dust, redstone, gunpowder, spider eyes, sugar, and sticks (except for sticks, all are potion ingredients).

Witches spawn in and around witch huts, typically found in swamps. They look like villagers garbed in witch gear.

They attack by throwing potions and can use healing potions on themselves, making them a tricky mob to face. Using a bow and arrow will keep you out of range of their attacks.

■ NETHER MOBS

Some mobs are found only in the Nether. They drop items impossible to get elsewhere, such as wither skulls (needed to summon a whither) and ghast tears (required in some potions).

WITHER SKELETONS

Drops: Bones, coal, stone swords, and wither skulls.

Wither skeletons are a darker version of their topside cousins. They are found in Nether fortresses and are more challenging to fight, because being hit by them causes the *wither effect*, which weakens the player for 10 seconds after being hit.

Very rarely, a wither skeleton will drop its skull, which is needed if you want to call the wither boss (see the "Bosses" section).

Wither skeletons are challenging to fight. They often spawn near a blaze, leaving you vulnerable to a double attack. It is best not to face them alone unless you are well equipped and have had combat practice.

BLAZE

Drops: Blaze rods (an excellent fuel choice for furnaces and an ingredient in potions).

Blaze are spinning, floating, fiery mobs that spawn only in Nether fortresses. They shoot balls of fire and can be tricky to fight. Using heat-resist potions and armor will help you withstand their attacks. They are vulnerable to water, but water evaporates in the Nether, so you need an alternative. Snowballs are the best weapon against a blaze (and fun too!).

GHASTS

Drops: Ghast tears and gunpowder.

Ghasts are large floating mobs that appear in the Nether. They shoot fireballs from a distance, so a bow is the best weapon when fighting them. They are not hard to conquer—what you need to be aware of is the terrain, because they are often over pools of lava. While watching for fireballs, you might not be paying attention to where you place your feet!

Ghast tears are a rare potion ingredient, making fighting ghasts worthwhile.

MAGMA CUBES

Drops: Magma cream.

Magma cubes are the Nether equivalent of slimes. Like slimes, they bounce around (they can also stretch out like springs), and they divide into smaller cubes when struck. Not every cube will drop cream. They are easy and worthwhile to fight, because magma cream is needed for heat-resist potions.

PLAYER-CREATED MOBS

Players can create a couple of mobs that in turn are loyal to those players. They help defend against hostile mobs and can be pets.

SNOW GOLEMS

Drops: Snowballs.

Snow golems are created by stacking two blocks of snow and then putting a pumpkin on top. This is done not on a crafting bench but in the game itself. They will animate and move around, leaving a trail of snow behind them. Ostensibly created as a defender, they will throw snowballs at most hostile mobs but won't do a lot of damage, other than knocking the hostile mob back.

You can also use snow golems to harvest snow and snowballs.

IRON GOLEMS

Drops: Iron ingots and roses.

Iron golems are far more powerful than snow golems. They can spawn spontaneously around NPC villages, but they can also be created. Like snow golems, iron golems are crafted right in the game but with four blocks of iron and a pumpkin for the head.

Iron golems will stay close to villages and protect villagers before players. They carry roses, which they offer to the villagers. When they attack, they are fierce—they are one of the most powerful mobs in the game. They swing their arms and will fling enemies a good distance, doing a lot of damage in the process. Their primary goal is to protect villagers, and if a player hits a villager, for whatever reason, the iron golem will attack the player.

Some players farm iron golems (by creating an empty village for them to spawn in) and then kill them for their iron.

■ BOSSES

There are currently two large, very powerful mobs known as *bosses*: withers, which can be summoned after collecting three wither skeleton heads, and the ender dragon, which spawns in the End.

WITHERS

Drops: Nether star.

A Nether star is a rare item that is needed to light a beacon, a special beam of light that extends to the sky and provides a special effect (such as speed) to all the players in an area. The only way to collect a Nether star is to kill a wither.

A wither must be summoned using a soul sand cross and three wither skeleton skulls. There is an order and pattern to the summoning; the last block placed must be a skull.

Taking the form of a three-headed floating monster, the wither attacks by shooting exploding skulls from all three of its heads. This barrage is hard to deflect and has a blast radius that delivers what is known as the *wither effect*. Some of the skulls will damage the blocks in the area, and if a player is directly hit by a skull, the wither will regain some health points.

Fighting a wither is a huge undertaking. It is best faced with several players if you are on a multiplayer server (and in that situation, it can be a lot of fun).

ENDER DRAGON

Drops: Dragon egg.

Only found in the End, which is populated by endermen, the ender dragon swoops in to attack players and can do damage with its head, wings, and body. Its head is the most vulnerable place for players to strike.

Unlike most other mobs, the ender dragon has a health bar, so you can see the damage it has been dealt. You can also see the health increase as it comes into contact with the ender crystals that are scattered around the End. A good strategy is to break the ender crystals before going on the attack, preventing the dragon from healing itself. Be careful of where you are in relation to it. Not only can the dragon injure players, but it will explode blocks as it flies by—you don't want to be in the blast radius.

WHAT TO DO IN MINECRAFT

When you first start a game, the lack of direction can be overwhelming. You'll require a few basics, though—food and shelter being the most important. Building a simple home and starting a farm are good first steps. Then do some exploring and mining to acquire building materials, after which you can experiment with building, crafting, using redstone, and all the other fun things you can do in the game.

A Minecraft world offers scads of resources. Some are found or mined, such as wood and ores, while others, such as various types of meat, are dropped by animal mobs. Carrots and potatoes are consumable as found, and wheat and sugar cane must be crafted into edible foods. There are also plenty of tools, building materials, weapons, books, and potions.

Some items are usable as they first appear; others, like iron, must be smelted in a furnace first. Many items must be crafted, sometimes in multiple steps—bookshelves, for example, are crafted using wood and books, which in turn need to be crafted from paper made with reeds, and leather.

Items change with each update, and in many cases have several properties or uses. Here is a brief summary of the more common items, divided into categories.

Before we get into the specifics of farming, mining, and building, let's take a look at the basic blocks and materials.

■ BLOCKS

In Minecraft, blocks are the most basic material. They come in a huge variety of types, from stones and ores to wool and wood. Blocks are approximately a meter long on each side, and they can be collected, harvested, or mined and then placed or used to craft other items. Some materials, such as wood and some types of stone, can be crafted into half slabs or stairs, which adds the ability to incorporate different design elements into your builds.

A huge part of the fun of Minecraft is experimenting with materials and learning how to use and craft with them. There are far more types of blocks (well over a hundred) than we can cover here, and many more ways to craft and create with them. Encourage your children to explore the materials. Working in Creative mode allows them to see exactly how many blocks there are, without having to find or craft them.

Crafting things from base materials is easy as long as you have a crafting bench (see Chapter 5) and know the recipe. Let's look at some of the basic block materials.

WOOD

When you start a game, one of the first things you need to do is gather wood with which to make a crafting bench and basic tools. At the time I'm writing this, the game offers four types of trees: oak, birch, spruce, and jungle wood (**Figure 6.8**). While they differ in appearance, they share similar properties. All trees drop saplings when they are chopped down. Saplings can be planted in dirt to grow more trees (applying bone meal from skeleton mob drops makes them grow almost instantaneously). Oak trees also drop apples, and cocoa beans grow only on jungle wood.

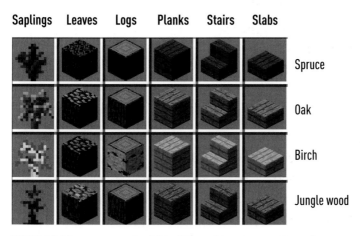

Saplings	Leaves	Logs	Planks	Stairs	Slabs	
						Spruce
						Oak
						Birch
						Jungle wood

FIGURE 6.8 The appearance of the different trees as saplings, leaves, logs, and wood

When you chop down a tree, either with your bare hands (often called punching a tree) or with an axe (once you've made one), you'll get logs. You can build with these, or you can turn them into planks and sticks, which can be crafted into a variety of objects, from chests and crafting benches to building materials such as doors, fences, trap doors, and stairs. The wood can also be used as fuel for a furnace. When you turn wood into planks, each type of wood retains its unique appearance, which is great for building and design. But when you craft things from the wood, such as doors or fences, the appearance of the wood will be the same regardless of the type you started with.

Each type of tree grows a little differently—birch grows fastest, for instance, while jungle trees are much taller than other types. Future updates may include new types of trees.

DIRT, STONE, AND CLAY

Dirt, stone, and clay are some of the more readily available materials. Dirt, sand, and usually gravel don't change when they are gathered. (Gravel will sometimes become flint when you mine it.) Stone cracks and becomes cobblestone when collected. If you smelt cobblestone in a furnace, or use a special pick that you've enchanted with silk touch, the stone becomes smooth stone once more. Smooth stone can be combined to form stone bricks (**Figure 6.9**).

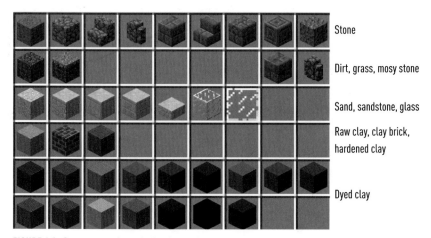

FIGURE 6.9 Stone, sand, and clay in various states

Clay can be found underwater, especially in swamps. When gathered, it breaks into four smaller balls, which can be placed in a furnace to create clay bricks. Once baked, these bricks can be combined to form clay brick blocks. You can also make flowerpots from clay bricks and place plants in them for decoration. Four clay balls can be reformed into a clay block, which, once hardened in a furnace, can be dyed into one of 16 muted colors. This makes clay incredibly versatile.

Sand and sandstone are found in deserts, and sand is also found on beaches and at the bottom of bodies of water. Sand and gravel don't stay where they are placed because they are affected by gravity. If you are digging above your head, sand will fall on you and smother you, so care must be taken. When smelted, sand forms glass blocks, which can be made into glass panes. Previews of the 1.7 update show that it will be possible to use dye on glass, creating 16 colors of stained glass.

Use a shovel for dirt, sand, gravel, and clay, and a pick for all types of stone.

ORES

You can find and mine many types of ore, from simple and plentiful coal to jewels such emeralds and diamonds (**Figure 6.10**). All ores start as blocks, though coal, redstone, lapis lazuli, emerald, diamond, and Nether quartz break into small pieces when mined. These smaller ore pieces can be formed into blocks on a crafting bench, using nine pieces of ore for one block.

Gold and iron must be smelted in a furnace, creating gold and iron ingots, which can be combined to form blocks. One gold bar can be divided into nine nuggets, which are needed for a variety of recipes, including golden carrots and apples.

You can enchant tools such as picks by using your experience points and an enchanting table. If you have a silk-touch–enchanted pick, you can mine ores without breaking them into smaller pieces.

A pick with a fortune enchantment will cause each of the ore blocks other than gold and iron to drop multiple pieces. (See the "Enchanting" section for more information.)

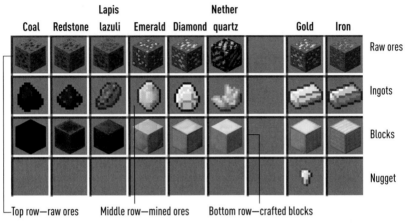

FIGURE 6.10 Breakable ores, gold, and iron in their various states

Use a pick for all of these ores. While you can use a stone pick to mine coal, lapis lazuli, iron, and Nether quartz, you'll need to smelt and craft an iron pick to mine redstone, gold, emeralds, and diamonds. A diamond pick is strongest and will allow you to mine longer and more efficiently (it takes fewer hits to break extract the ore), and enchanted tools are the best. We'll look more at this in the section on tools.

ORGANIC BLOCKS

You can build using all sorts of blocks that wouldn't typically be considered building materials (**Figure 6.11**). This includes wool (which can be dyed 16 colors), food such as watermelon and pumpkins, leaves from trees, and snow and ice blocks. These all add visual variety to your structures, and some have additional features. Pumpkins, for example, when combined in a crafting bench with a torch, become lit jack-o'-lanterns, which can be used for lighting.

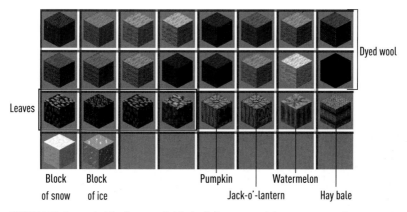

FIGURE 6.11 Organic blocks are viable building materials.

OTHER ITEMS

While blocks are the building material in Minecraft, many other items have building or decorative functions (**Figure 6.12**).

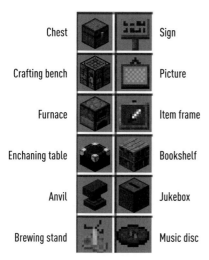

FIGURE 6.12 Craftable items

All these craftable items require recipes to build them, and most will need to be assembled on a crafting bench. For example, a bed, which is one of the first things you'll need if you build away from your spawn point, is crafted from wood and wool; and to travel on water, you'll need to build boats, using five planks (**Figure 6.13**). Some iron items, such as doors, require that you mine and then smelt the iron into bars before crafting them. The Minecraft wiki is the best place to go for recipes, but I suggest you or your kids have fun laying out materials on a crafting bench and experiementing.

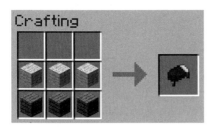 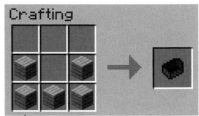

FIGURE 6.13 The recipes for crafting a bed and a boat.

■ TOOLS

To acquire building materials, you need tools. You'll want to craft basic tools, like a shovel and pickaxe, right away; others, such as a fishing rod, are more for entertainment purposes (though you need to catch fish if you want to tame cats).

Tools are constructed on a crafting bench. Most tools have a wooden handle made from wood sticks, and the appropriate head (shovel, pick axe) can be made from wood, stone, gold, iron, or diamond.

All tools, no matter the material, wear down with use. When you start to use a tool (and this applies to armor as well), a meter will appear on the tool in your inventory. This meter measures the tool's durability. Wooden tools are the least durable, diamond the most. Tools used on a block that isn't suitable for that tool (for instance, using an axe to mine stone) will wear out faster. Tools can be enchanted on an enchanting table by using experience points, and you might get an unbreaking enchantment that will extend the life of your tool. You can repair and name tools on an anvil, but this takes both experience points and more of the material you used to craft your tool. Because of the cost in experience points, most people save their enchantments for iron or diamond tools, which have the best endurance.

Tools also have varying levels of efficiency—how many hits it takes to break a block. Diamond and iron are more efficient than wood, stone, or gold. Efficiency enchantments can increase the effectiveness of a tool.

The steps for making tools are broken down for you in Chapter 5. The same steps apply to all tools—the only difference is the recipe, the pattern they fit into on the crafting bench.

Figure 6.14 shows recipes for the basic tools you'll need: axe, hoe, shovel, and pick. For further recipes, check the wiki.

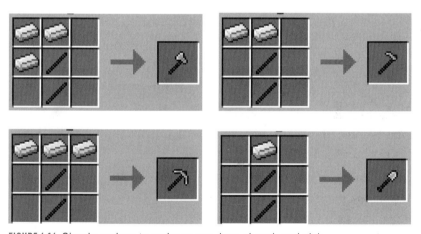

FIGURE 6.14 Simple recipes to make an axe, hoe, shovel, and pick

■ WEAPONS AND ARMOR

To me, weapons and armor are simply other types of tool. I can use a sword and bow to collect food and items from animals even in a peaceful game. Armor protects me, especially when I enchant it, giving me added protection from mobs and fire.

WEAPONS

Swords are crafted with a wooden stick and wood, stone, gold, iron, or diamond. The properties are the same as for tools—iron and diamond last longer and are better than wood, stone, or gold. Swords can be given such enchantments as sharpness, flame, and looting. Bows and arrows can be collected from skeletons or crafted. Bows can be enchanted as well, giving them greater distance and power or infinite arrows, meaning need to carry only one arrow in your inventory.

ARMOR

Armor consists of four pieces: helmet, chest or chest plate, leggings, and boots (**Figure 6.15**). You can make armor from leather, gold, iron, and diamond, following the same laws of durability as for tools. Different pieces of armor can take different enchantments: *feather fall* goes on boots to let you fall a greater distance without damage, for example, and *respiration* goes on helmets and allows you to remain under water longer. Like tools, armor wears out and will need to be repaired or replaced.

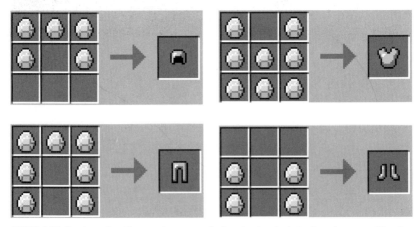

FIGURE 6.15 Recipes for diamond armor—helmet, chest plate, leggings, and boots.

You equip, or wear, armor by pressing E to open your inventory and dragging the armor to the appropriate slots beside your crafting grid (**Figure 6.16**).

When you are wearing armor, an armor bar will appear above your heart meter (**Figure 6.17**).

Helmet

Chest plate

Leggings

Boots

FIGURE 6.16 Wearing your armor is as easy as dragging it to the appropriate slot in your inventory.

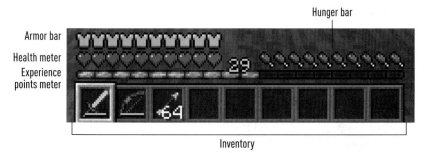

Armor bar

Health meter

Experience points meter

Hunger bar

Inventory

FIGURE 6.17 Your armor meter will appear automatically above your heart meter if you put on armor.

The type and quality of your armor will affect how much of the armor meter is filled. Damage taken during combat or through falls or fire will deplete your armor durability.

Chainmail is an uncraftable type of armor that you can get from zombies and in village trades. It is somewhere between gold and iron for durability and defense.

ENCHANTING

Enchanting is an involved activity, so I'm just going to touch upon it here. You and your kids won't be enchanting until you've been playing for a while, and by then you'll likely have discovered some favorite resources to seek more information specific to your needs and questions. You can enchant tools, armor, weapons, and books. You can apply the enchantments of enchanted books to items by using an anvil and some experience points (**Figure 6.18**).

FIGURE 6.18 An enchanting table will allow you to place a variety of enchantments on your items.

EXPERIENCE POINTS

Experience points are gained through killing mobs (including friendly mobs like cows and pigs), mining ores, smelting items in a furnace, and breeding animals. They are lost when you die or when you use them to enchant an item. More advanced players make what are called *mob grinders*, using mob spawners found in dungeons. *Grinding* is a gaming term for doing the same mindless and repetitive action, usually to gain experience points.

The designs of mob grinders vary, but the basic concept is the player builds a room around a mob spawner and then guides the mobs to an area where they take damage and then are killed by the player, releasing the mobs' experience points. YouTube is full of designs for zombies, skeletons, blazes, and even enderman grinders, and this is something to explore once you or your kids have been playing a while.

ENCHANTING TABLE

Enchanting is done using an enchanting table and experience points. To craft one, you need diamonds and obsidian, as well as a book (**Figure 6.19**).

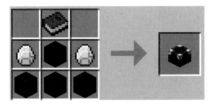

FIGURE 6.19 Crafting an enchanting table

To enchant an object, click the enchanting table and place the item you'd like enchanted in the item box (**Figure 6.20**). Enchantments come in levels, from 1 to 30, though you need to surround your enchanting table with bookshelves to make it strong enough to provide level-30 enchantments. You cannot select a specific enchantment. Select the enchantment level by clicking the appropriate bar, and as long as you have enough experience points a random enchantment will be applied to your tool, weapon, armor, or book. The enchantment is permanently applied when you pick up your item.

FIGURE 6.20 When you use an enchanting table, you choose the enchantment level you'd like to use.

ANVIL

You craft an anvil with iron bars and blocks (**Figure 6.21**). You use an anvil to repair tools and armor, either by combining two matching tools or pieces of armor or by combining the damaged piece with raw material or an enchanted book. You can also give items names with an anvil. All these actions require experience points, however.

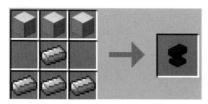

FIGURE 6.21 You need an anvil to repair and name items.

To use an anvil, right-click it and then place the item to be repaired in the first box. In the second box, place a second one of the same item, an enchanted book (**Figure 6.22**), or raw materials. You'll be told how many experience points the repair will cost (anvils can go as high as 39 experience points, after which it says the repair is "too expensive"), and you see from the bar on the item whether it will be fully or partially repaired. The repair is finished when you pick the item up. When you combine two enchanted items, the enchantments are combined on the repaired item.

FIGURE 6.22 When you add an enchantment to an item—such as using an enchanted book on an unenchanted sword—the enchanted item will glow.

POTIONS

Brewing potions is an advanced part of the game. You need time and skill to gather many of the ingredients, but it can also be a lot of fun and worth the effort. Potions come in two forms: splash potions (which you throw and which affect the person or mob that they splash on) and bottled potions (which you ingest). Potions such as weakness, slowing, and harm are used on enemies. You use strength, speed, night vision, and healing potions on yourself (or splash on yourself and allies if you stand close together).

To brew potions, you need to craft a brewing stand, which requires a blaze rod, and which in turn means that you have to have explored the Nether before you can really consider crafting potions (**Figure 6.23**).

FIGURE 6.23 A brewing stand

■ FARMING

Food is a vital part of Minecraft. You need to eat, so you need to collect or harvest food. You can find some food as you wander (in the form of animals you meet or the occasional apple), but it's much easier to set up a farm and grow and harvest your own food.

When you start a game, food is a priority and almost an obsession. As you play, create, and work your farm, chances are high you'll end up with far more food than you know what to do with.

Much of the food in Minecraft can be found in its natural state, and much can be planted and grown easily (carrots, potatoes, melons). Some food is in the form of mobs (cows, chickens, pigs). Specialty foods are crafted (cookies, cakes, pies). It's good to live somewhere near where animals spawn, because you'll have a food source, but it's still easier to create a farm, grow crops, and breed your own animals.

Farms can be of any size. **Figure 6.24** shows a compact farm with reeds, pumpkins, carrots, potatoes, and melons, as well as a horse pasture and barn in the background.

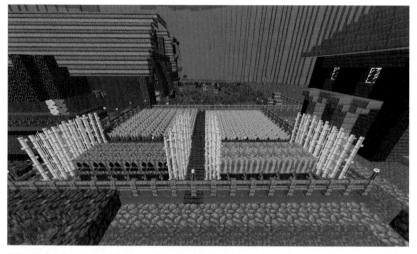

FIGURE 6.24 A compact farm

LIVESTOCK

Be sure to check out the "Mobs" section for information on breeding various animals. You can make and use leads to bring your animals to your farm. To breed, all you need is a pair of each kind of animal you'd like to have, and you can breed the rest from there.

Keep your livestock in fenced pens or barns. You can have a lot of fun with designing your space. You can keep animals underground too, but remember that sheep will only regrow their wool when they eat grass, so you'll need to use a silk-touch shovel or pick to dig up a grass block. Plant grass among dirt blocks and give it enough light, and it will spread.

CROPS

To grow basic crops, you need dirt, water, crop seeds, and a hoe. Crops will grow without a water source, but they will develop very slowly. Ideally, you want all your crops to be within four squares of a water source. This can be either a channel of water running through your garden or water under the ground. There are tons of ways to lay out each individual crop, including using sophisticated crop-harvesting mechanisms (**Figure 6.25**).

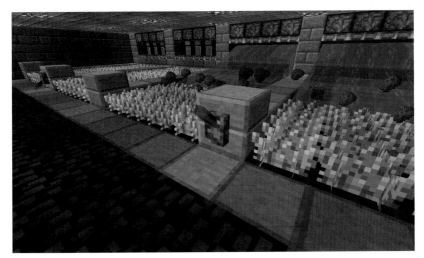

FIGURE 6.25 Automated farms use redstone circuits and switches. Here, the flip of a lever sends water over the crops, harvesting them in a flash, though they still need to be replanted by hand.

Lay out your plot of land, making sure you have a water source (this is where buckets come in handy). Use a hoe to till the soil—the area will flatten a small amount. Plant your seeds by right-clicking them—they will take some time to grow. If you're in a hurry, you can use bonemeal, made by placing bones in a crafting table. Place bonemeal on each crop to speed it through its growth cycle. When the crop is fully grown, left-click it to harvest. Crops such as carrots and potatoes will yield more than one plant per square, giving you extras to plant. Others, such as wheat, will give you seeds for replanting.

Common crops include carrots and potatoes, both of which are occasionally dropped by zombies but are also found in villager gardens. You plant the entire carrot or potato, and you harvest when you can see the tops of the new ones poking through the earth under the leaves. Carrots can be eaten whole; potatoes give you more energy when they are baked in a furnace. Potatoes that are poisoned have a greenish hue—don't eat those!

Wheat, melons, and pumpkins grow from seeds. Melon seeds can be found in chests in dungeons and abandoned mineshafts or through trading with villagers, as melons don't grow in the wild, but pumpkins can be found scattered across plains, forest, and other biomes, and harvested for seeds. Wheat is useful not just for breeding animals but for making bread and other recipes. You can get wheat seeds from cutting long grass. Hoe your dirt blocks, and plant your wheat. When it is tall and has a brownish tinge it is ready for harvest. Wheat will give you seeds as well as wheat stalks, and wheat stalks can be made into bales of hay.

■ MINING

Mining is an important part of Minecraft. You need to mine to obtain many materials, particularly ores (such as diamonds, from which you can make better tools) and redstone (which you need for circuits). You also gather stone as you mine, and it is through mining that you find dungeons and abandoned mineshafts.

Some people find mining to be incredibly boring (though I find it relaxing); at the same time, it can be dangerous, particularly for new players. The bulk of my Minecraft deaths have occurred while mining, mostly from lava. And when you die in lava, your items burn, so you won't be able to recover them.

You need to be well prepared so you can mine as long as you like without having to get more food or supplies. Be sure to bring plenty of food, a couple of stacks of torches, two or three buckets of water, a chest and crafting bench, some wood to make more torches, chests or handles for tools, a shovel for dirt and gravel, a couple of picks, armor, and a sword. You need at least an iron pick to mine diamonds.

WHERE TO MINE

In mining, the ultimate goal is usually to find diamonds. Along the way you'll come across plenty of coal, redstone, iron, other ores, and stone.

Diamonds typically appear between levels 0 (bedrock) and 16. Between levels 10 and 15 is a good area to aim for, but to get there, you need to know how to tell how deep you are. Remember that pressing F3 will give you game information, including your coordinates. Coordinates in Minecraft are found on the x, y, and z lines—x and z run perpendicular to each other, x is east-west, and z is north-south. That leaves the y axis, which runs up and down starting at 0 (the bedrock, or stone base, of a Minecraft map).

The quickest and easiest way to reach the lower levels is to mine a staircase, descending one block at a time. You can also experiment with making a spiral staircase, or you could even dig straight down, placing ladders as you go.

As you dig, be wary of lava. If you keep your volume turned up, you should be able to hear it. It sounds a little like water. You need to be aware of it, because you might end up mining right into a lava pool (**Figure 6.26**).

FIGURE 6.26 As you mine, you'll find pools of lava in open caves—be careful!

MINING METHODS

There are lots of ways to mine—you can dig in a straight line until you reach the end of the map, a cavern, or an abandoned mineshaft. Or you can dig shorter tunnels. Digging tunnels that are two or three blocks high and one or two blocks wide is pretty standard, though some people make them only one block wide. Bring torches and remember to place them often so you can follow them to your home and keep mobs from spawning in your tunnel.

To branch-mine, dig a long, straight tunnel as your main mine-shaft, and then branch out and dig paths on either side. A good rule of thumb is to leave two or three blocks between tunnels.

People have lots of tricks to keep them from getting lost. When you only have one tunnel this might seem silly, but as you add more, you can get turned around. Placing stone block markers is a good idea; you could even make and bring signs. A simple technique is to put torches only on the right-side wall as you dig. That way you can always check whether you're going the correct way; when it's time to find your way out, just keep the torches to your left. If you find yourself in an underground cave or abandoned mineshaft, you'll be glad that you used a system.

CREATING A BASE CAMP

At the head of your mine, create a base camp (**Figure 6.27**). Your base camp should contain a crafting bench, a chest or two, food, and tools, as well as the ores and stone you mine. Place your chest and drop about half of what you're carrying in it, in case you die and can't retrieve your belongings—you'll be able to return here and recover your stores. Also leave half your torches and food, any spare tools, and anything you don't actively need.

Chest   Crafting bench   Furnace   Torch

FIGURE 6.27 A small base camp with a chest, crafting bench, and furnace

You could place a bed in your base camp so that if you die, you'll respawn in the mine (remember to "sleep" in it to set it as your new spawn point). If you'd like to smelt your iron, gold, or cobblestone while you work, place a furnace (or several) here as well.

Your base camp should be accessible and easy to find. Write down the coordinates (press F3 or use a map mod, as described in Chapter 7) in case you get turned around or travel too far. You might also want to carry a chest as you mine so that if you find precious ores you can drop them off while you keep mining. Just don't lose track of all the cool things you find!

If you don't have a silk touch–enchanted pick yet, all the stone you dig will turn to cobble, but you can turn it back to smooth stone in a furnace. Build some furnaces in your base, and when you find coal, use it to smelt your cobblestone.

You'll also find gravel and sand underground; for both of these, use a shovel. Be careful that the gravel doesn't smother you—it falls, so you could end up buried.

AVOIDING TROUBLE

The most hazardous thing you'll find is lava. If you break through to lava above your floor level, it will pour through the opening toward you. You'll need to back up fast! Use whichever stone blocks you have at hand to block the lava so it stops flowing toward you. Then you have a few options: You can leave it and mine in another direction; you can block it with stone; you can drop gravel on it to absorb the lava (keep adding more gravel until it piles to the surface of the lava, giving you a path to walk on); or you can pour water on it, which will turn it into obsidian. If you use water, make sure you scoop the water back up with your bucket, because you might need it again. These methods take some practice, because when lava is pouring toward you your first reaction is panic. Practice before you go mining, and don't rush as you dig. When you're near lava, you can press the left-Shift button to crouch—this also prevents you from falling and lets you extend your reach past the edge of the block you're on.

If you break through to a cavern, you can often go exploring for quite some distance. This is a good way to find exposed ore in the cavern walls, but keep an eye open for mobs too—they particularly like dark caverns. You might also find yourself in an abandoned mineshaft filled with tunnels, bridges, mine cart tracks, chests, and spawners. Mineshafts, with their multiple levels, can be easy to get lost in, so make sure to mark your coordinates.

As you mine, items will stack in your inventory, and at some point you'll need to run back to your chest to drop things off. Do this anytime you find valuable ore. If you find diamond, store it back at your base right away in case you have an unfortunate accident. And when you're starting out, you might want to store your iron and coal right away too. Later, you'll likely find that you have plenty, but it takes a while to create a stockpile.

When you find diamond, before you mine it, carefully dig all up all the blocks around it. Diamonds can often be near lava, and if you don't check you might accidentally strike into lava and lose what you've mined. This preventative step can save you much frustration.

Once you've been playing and mining for a bit, you'll have some strategies of your own, and you'll be ready to create more elaborate mines and explore caverns and abandoned mineshafts.

■ NEXT STEPS

Once you have an understanding of the basics, there is so much more to do. Much will be dependent on your children's interests. Some will want to farm and may spend hours exploring and experimenting with automated farms, breeding horses, or collecting dye for sheep, clay, and fireworks—which is my personal specialty, and what I sell on our server. Others become explorers, learn to navigate on foot and sea, and perhaps try their hand at building powered railways to connect distant places or traverse from their home to their mine. Still others might become mining experts or master builders. Many of these skills will require them to try their hand at redstone circuitry.

Redstone circuitry is a fascinating and at times challenging aspect of Minecraft—whether it's to make a time-delayed door or a massive music box. Combining redstone powder, switches, levers, pistons, or other electronic devices, your children can build simple or fairly complex circuits.

Now that you have the basic tools and understanding at your command, it's time to get on the computer and put what you've read into practice—or at least hang out with your kids and see what they're up to. You might surprise them with your sudden knowledge. Play, explore, experiment, and research further—the world of Minecraft is ever growing, ever expanding, and ever so much fun!

CHAPTER 7

DIGGING DEEPER: TECHNICAL SPECIFICS

MINECRAFT IS CONSTANTLY evolving and changing. The programmers at Mojang release updates that can add dozens of changes at a time, and the players themselves create endless texture packs, resource packs, and modifications. All these can be found online and installed by anyone. The process can be frustrating to those with limited computer skills, but it is easier if you break the installation into steps.

Because mods are written by individuals, there are many ways to install them. The most basic method is to download them and then add them to a folder inside the Minecraft folder, but other methods use a special mod loader. In this chapter I touch on the basics, introduce some mods, and tell you where to find others.

THE MINECRAFT FOLDER

Minecraft is stored in a folder on your computer. Any mods or resource packs you add go into folders within the Minecraft folder. Until recently, to make changes to texture packs or add mods, you needed to navigate your way through these folders. Mojang is slowly changing this by creating their own API (application programming interface). For the lay person, this doesn't mean much, except that it will become easier to add and change resource packs and mods. It's unclear how things will develop, so I'll advise you in the following sections if you might need to look for updated information.

Here's how to access your Minecraft files.

▦ WINDOWS

1. Open the Run window, either through the Start menu or by pressing Control+R on your keyboard.

2. In the Open field, type **%appdata%**, and click OK (**Figure 7.1**). You'll see a list of folders.

3. Open the .minecraft folder (**Figure 7.2**). You'll see all the folders related to your game, including mods, resource packs, and screenshots.

FIGURE 7.1 Accessing your Minecraft folder through the Run command

Name	Date modified	Type	Size
assets	2013-09-12 12:49 AM	File folder	
config	2013-09-19 10:47 AM	File folder	
crash-reports	2013-08-28 2:34 AM	File folder	
libraries	2013-09-12 12:51 AM	File folder	
magic	2013-08-05 10:07 AM	File folder	
mods	2013-09-19 10:47 AM	File folder	
resourcepacks	2013-09-12 1:12 AM	File folder	
resources	2013-09-19 10:47 AM	File folder	
saves	2013-09-18 11:18 AM	File folder	
schematics	2013-09-20 1:35 PM	File folder	
screenshots	2013-09-26 8:49 PM	File folder	
shaderpacks	2013-09-17 9:31 PM	File folder	
stats	2013-09-26 10:00 PM	File folder	
versions	2013-09-12 12:49 AM	File folder	

FIGURE 7.2 The .minecraft folder contains all the folders and files pertaining to your game.

OS X

In recent releases of OS X, including OS X 10.9 Mavericks, Apple has hidden the Library folder. No worries. You can still uncover it.

1. In the Finder, press and hold the Option key as you click the Go menu and select Library (**Figure 7.3**).

2. Open the Application Support folder.

3. Navigate to the minecraft folder (**Figure 7.4**).

FIGURE 7.3 Accessing the Library

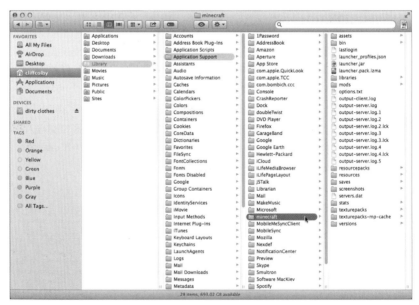

FIGURE 7.4 On a Mac, you can find the minecraft folder inside the Application Support folder.

SKINS, RESOURCE PACKS, AND MODS

You have several ways to change your game in Minecraft. Skins and texture packs make simple visual changes, whereas mods can change the way the game is played.

SKINS

Your skin in Minecraft is the way your character appears. Finding or creating a skin is easy and is something even the youngest players want to do. Everyone starts out with the standard "Steve" skin, but it's fun to change what you look like.

If you want to create your own skin, there are websites set up for exactly that, or you can use a program like Microsoft Paint. You can upload your skins to share with other players.

There are thousands of skins to choose from, from characters in popular shows and books to seasonal skins or monsters.

Playing with skin creation can lead to hours of exploration. My current skin is a combination of a skin I found online and my own first forays into creating skins. It's like shopping for clothes—my hair and face are unique, but I found my clothes online, although I did change the colors of my clothes and the logo on my T-shirt. Some players change skins regularly, while others stick with one.

INSTALLING A NEW SKIN

Installing a skin is as easy as finding one you like, downloading it, and then uploading it to your Minecraft profile. And many sites even take out that intermediate step of downloading—they take you directly to your Minecraft.net profile so that you can upload your skin immediately.

There are many sites where you can find, edit, and create skins. The Skindex (minecraftskins.com) (**Figure 7.5** on the next page) and Novaskin (minecraft.novaskin.me) (**Figure 7.6** on the next page) have thousands of skins to choose from. Both allow you to edit your chosen skin, or create one from scratch. Although they share many features, I find the Skindex easier to use but also more limited. Your best bet is to show the sites to your child and just let them play around and experiment (and you can too!). Save their creations so they can go back and forth between skins if they'd like. And if you don't want to create a custom skin, you can quickly find a skin you like and upload it without editing.

FIGURE 7.5 The default skin for Minecraft is "Steve," shown here on the Skindex page.

Changing your skin to a pre-existing skin is simple and similar using either site.

1. Make sure Minecraft is closed.

2. Go to either minecraftskins.com or minecraft.novaskin.me. If you would like to save your skins on the site, create an account following the site directions.

FIGURE 7.6 Novaskin allows you to look up skins by player name.

3. Browse the available skins by using keywords, or just explore the gallery of skins.

4. Locate a skin you want. On Skindex, click Upload To Minecraft; on Novaskin, click Apply. You will be taken to your Minecraft profile.

5. Enter the email address and password for the account for which you want to change the skin. You'll be taken to the Change Your Skin screen (**Figure 7.7**).

FIGURE 7.7 Changing your skin is a simple process.

6. Click the Change button, and your skin will be uploaded. This might take a minute or two. The next time you log in to Minecraft, the new skin will be on your character.

EDITING OR CREATING A SKIN

If you prefer a unique skin, you can use Skindex or Novaskin (or any other skin editor) to modify your existing skin or create one from scratch. Skins are created using pixelated squares with a grid placed over the character. Skin editors have tools much like you'd find in a paint program, such as color palettes, painting tools, and shading and color-matching features. Even if these are completely new to you, chances are high that they are not new to your kids, who are likely to have used paint programs at school. And even if it's brand new to them, with some experimenting you'll quickly figure it out. The Skindex and Novaskin sites have tips and FAQs, and you can find tutorials online.

Some quick pointers:

- On some programs, the skin grid is laid flat, showing what the skin would look like on a piece of paper.

- If you're creating a skin, you only need to create one arm and one leg—do one and the other will fill in to match.

- When working on a 3D character, you can spin the character by dragging it with the mouse to work on the sides, back, top of the head, and bottom of the feet.

- Play with the shading and gradient tools—they can add some fun details.

TEXTURE AND RESOURCE PACKS

Texture packs are like skins for all the blocks in the game. With them, you can change the appearance the game, from the blocks to the mobs, armor, and items. Premade texture packs are designed so that the blocks are still the same but their appearance is vastly different. In a sci-fi texture pack, for instance, a block of yellow wool might look like a spaceship control panel. This allows for great creativity in designing themed builds. Texture packs can subtly or drastically change the way Minecraft appears. As you can see in **Figure 7.8**, the items in my inventory have different appearances because I used different texture packs.

Some texture packs focus on time periods, making your game look medieval or futuristic, while others are based on architectural themes. Many servers, like MineTrek, use custom texture packs, and will suggest you download them before you start to play. You can also create your own texture packs by using a texture pack program such as Novaskin or by using Adobe Photoshop or Microsoft Paint.

Recently, Mojang introduced resource packs, which allow you to change the game's sounds, music, and fonts. As part of the addition of resource packs, Mojang changed the way that texture packs are incorporated. The process of installing them has changed as well, so all current texture packs have had to be converted to fit the new resource packs, or users need to convert them with tools created by Mojang.

FIGURE 7.8 Texture packs (clockwise from upper left): Default Minecraft, Dokucraft TSC Light, LIFE, and Glimmar's Steampunk

Wrednax

I QUITE OFTEN USE TEXTURE PACKS. One of my favorites is Dokucraft. I like its fantasy style and that it has different texture packs for different themes, from high fantasy to the more nitty-gritty stuff. The Painterly Pack has its own customizer where you can change what every block looks like, so that "takes the cake" customization-wise. I also really like the Last Days texture pack, because of its unique post-apocalyptic art style. And Glimmar's Steampunk texture pack will always have a special place in my heart because steampunk, with its meld of steam-powered technology and Victorian style, is something that I love (**Figure 7.9**).

FIGURE 7.9 Xander in some of his steampunk gear.

INSTALLING A TEXTURE PACK

Mojang is changing how texture packs and mods are added to the game, so the following directions are subject to change.

First you need to find a texture pack that you'd like to install. It's best to install one that has been updated to fit the current version of Minecraft. Minecraftforum.net and minecrafttexturepacks.com are likely to be up to date.

1. Select a texture pack to upload (**Figure 7.10**).

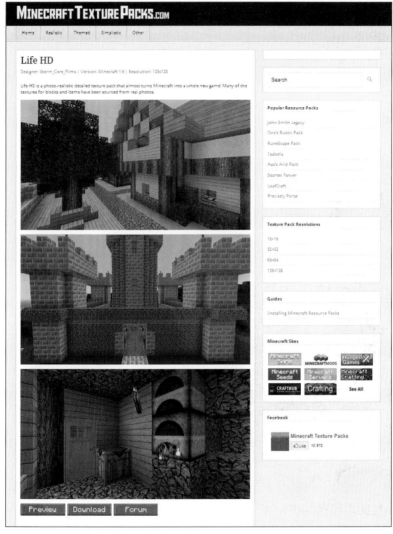

FIGURE 7.10 Selecting a texture pack is fun. Each one will change the appearance of your game.

2. Download the texture pack file. On most sites, simply click the Download button. The file will be zipped. Do not unzip it; place it on your desktop.

3. Open Minecraft. On the main page, click Options.

4. Click Resource Packs (**Figure 7.11**).

5. Click Open Resource Pack Folder at the bottom of the page (**Figure 7.12**).

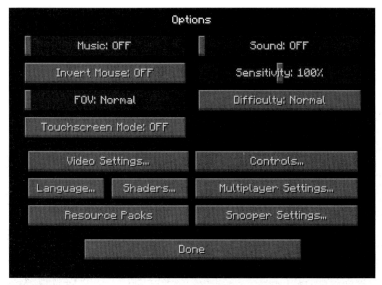

FIGURE 7.11 Resource packs can be accessed from the Options menu.

FIGURE 7.12 The Open Resource Pack Folder button allows you to easily access the resource pack you'd like to use.

6. Drag the zipped texture pack file into the resourcepacks folder
(**Figure 7.13**).

FIGURE 7.13 The resourcepacks folder in your .minecraft folder

7. The newly added texture pack will appear in the Resource Pack
menu (**Figure 7.14**). Simply click it to use it.

FIGURE 7.14 Once you've installed a texture pack or resource pack, you can easily
access it from the Resource Pack menu, which is in Minecraft's Options menu.

▓ MODS

Mods are program modifications that you can add to Minecraft to
change or enhance how you play. Some add different mobs, plants, or
items, and others add extra tools and commands. Some mods have a
specific, narrow function, such as Rei's Minimap, which allows you to set
waypoint markers (more on these later). Others can completely change
gameplay, such as Feed the Beast (FTB), which introduces Minecraft
high-level technology such as a mining laser and nuclear reactors.

There really are endless mods, which is part of what makes Minecraft so appealing. The game evolves as players create the changes and additions they'd like to see. And young people learn basic Java programming as they try their hand at creating mods, which opens doors to further programming exploration.

Mods are written by players, so they are not the property of Mojang. Mod creators are not always able to update at the same time as Minecraft does, so some mods may not work as described or may have bugs in the programming. As well, there is a risk of downloading a virus or malware with some mods, so make sure the mod you're downloading has positive reviews and comments.

I strongly recommend that you not allow your children to download and install mods on their own until you are confident in their computer skills, judgment, and ability to identify and deal with malware and viruses. I have known several families who have had computers ruined because of impulsive mod downloading. Educate your kids about how to find safe mods. Even Xander, who is very computer-savvy, accidentally downloaded a virus recently, from a program he'd used before without any trouble. Thankfully, he was able to deal with most of the problems on his own and knew who to ask for help when he needed it.

One good source for mods is minecraftforum.net. A large player base contributes to the forums, which means you can find comments and reviews for most of the mods. And there is a list of updated mods on the forums, so you can find mods that you know will run on the most recent version of Minecraft.

INSTALLING MODS

The system for installing mods has been changing, and it will change further when Mojang releases their new API. At the moment, most mods can be installed using either the Modloader or Forge API, which you'll need to download. You can find both at www.minecraftforum.net/. Some mods install quite easily; others can be frustrating. But thankfully the more popular ones have tutorials that players keep up to date.

Search online for up-to-date installation instructions for the mod you're interested in, and follow those directions. You can find basic directions on the Minecraft wiki, or you can search YouTube for a tutorial.

SELECTING MODS

Selecting a mod can be a challenge because there are so many available. I find that many kids enjoy the Mo' Creatures Mod, which adds mobs such as bunnies, scorpions, and wyvern to the game. The added variety of tamable pets and unique creatures makes this a fun mod to experiment with.

I use only a couple of mods, because our server does not allow mods that would give an unfair advantage to one player over another, but here are two that I find helpful.

OPTIFINE

OptiFine can drastically speed up and smooth out the game (**Figure 7.15** on the next page). If you are running Minecraft on an older computer or find that it lags when you are playing, give OptiFine a try. Even if your computer is fast, you can use OptiFine for smoother graphics. It updates regularly. You can find it on minecraftforums.net or through an online search. Some of its options include being able to turn off animations and weather, change your render settings, and use HD settings.

REI'S MINIMAP

I cannot do without Rei's Minimap, and I know many players who say the same. This map mod provides a small onscreen map and compass (and a large map at the push of a button), and it allows you to create markers, called *waypoints*, that help you find your way around. You can set waypoints at locations you'd like to mark—such as build sites or a mine you'd like to return to—and simply head for the markers when you want to return to them. You can also create a waypoint by entering the coordinates of a location, even if you've never been there; for example, if a friend would like you to visit their town on a multiplayer server (**Figure 7.16**).

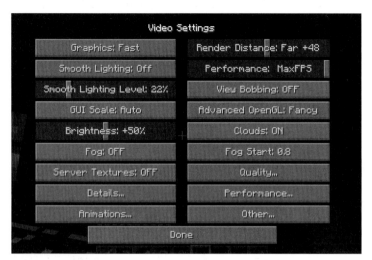

FIGURE 7.15 OptiFine has many options for changing game settings.

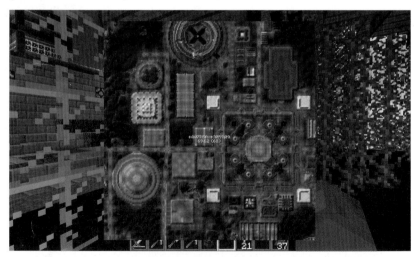

FIGURE 7.16 Rei's Minimap allows you to call up a map of your immediate area and set waypoints anywhere on the map.

These waypoints are extremely helpful to someone, like myself, who regularly gets lost. They show up on the map, and when they are turned on they appear on the horizon, allowing you to head directly for them without referring to your map. You can also turn on a death-points function, which automatically creates a waypoint when you die, so that you have a higher chance of reclaiming your items by allowing you to see precisely where you were killed. Of course, you still need to navigate there before your items despawn.

Wrednax

A LOT OF PEOPLE really like the Feed the Beast (FTB) modpack (a collective package of mods) because of its new crafting mechanism, different dimensions, extra biomes, and tons of different technological gizmos and magical devices. The best part about the modpack in my humble opinion is that it's designed for multiplayer, meaning you can play with your kid via a multiplayer server. I usually play on servers when playing FTB because I find it's more fun playing it when other people are around working on different projects. But this collection of mods is very complicated, so view some tutorials online. **Figure 7.17** shows a quarry that is powered by two combustion engines, which are being fed with fuel from a large tank.

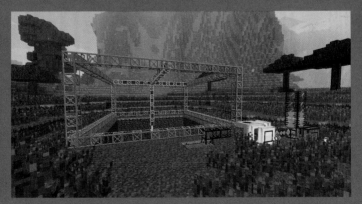

FIGURE 7.17 The Feed the Beast modpack

CHAPTER

PLAYING ON SERVERS

I AM GOING TO MAKE A BOLD PREDICTION and say that anyone who plays Minecraft for an extended period will end up playing with others via online servers. The online community is vast, the types of gameplay are growing, and there is much to be said for being part of an online community.

INTRODUCTION TO SERVERS

Gaming servers are websites where many players come together to play. There are hundreds of servers for Minecraft alone, with various themes and focuses. Some are family-friendly, some are very organized, and others are much more casual. Many are based on specific types of gameplay such as PVP (player versus player) or last-man-standing environments. Some host creative maps, others host survival maps, and some host both. Some servers are open to everyone, and some are *white-listed*, which means that only players with permission may play. There are endless themes as well, such as MineTrek, set in the future world of Star Trek, and Hogwarts, a Harry Potter–themed site.

Servers use *plugins* (software that changes or adds to the existing program) to change how the game is played. Plugins might allow for economies in games, add protection to parts of a world, or add extra commands; plugins work on the server side of the game, so they will not affect your computer in any way.

Servers are accessed by a unique address, such as an IP address or a unique name that you enter on the multiplayer screen, accessed through the main menu (**Figure 8.1**). You can find servers by word of mouth or by searching sites that list them. Many of these sites provide player ratings and comments about the servers, helping you narrow your search.

As a rule, playing on large, public servers should be reserved for older children and teens. Being able to read and type fluently are important, as is being able to navigate social situations and knowing when to seek help. Well-reviewed family-specific servers are the exception to this rule.

FIGURE 8.1 Minecraft provides an easy way to access multiplayer servers.

HOME SERVERS

The advantage of a home server is that you can control who plays on it. It might be a server just for your family, or you might choose to expand it to include friends or other families. When you host and run a server, you get to set the rules and decide how you want to enforce them. Setting up a small server for your neighborhood requires some computer skills, but setting up a LAN (local area network) server in your house is as easy as clicking a button in the game menu.

SETTING UP A LAN SERVER WITHIN MINECRAFT

Setting up a LAN server to play on the same Minecraft map—for others who are using the same Internet router—is incredibly easy.

1. Open a single-player game on one computer, and select a world to play on. This world will host the players (**Figure 8.2** on the next page).

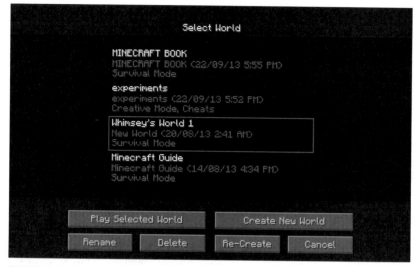

FIGURE 8.2 Select a world to be the host for your server.

2. Once in the game, press the Esc key on your keyboard to open the game menu, and click the Open to LAN button (**Figure 8.3**).

FIGURE 8.3 Click the Open to LAN button.

The LAN World page allows you to select what type of world you'd like (Survival, Creative, or Adventure) and whether you'd like to allow players to use cheat commands (**Figure 8.4**).

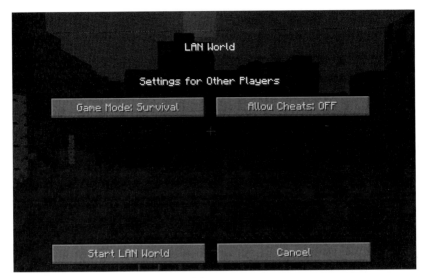

FIGURE 8.4 Basic options for your world

3. Make your selections and click the Start LAN World button.

You will get an in-game message that states "Local game hosted on port #####" (**Figure 8.5**).

FIGURE 8.5 Once you start your LAN server, you will receive a port number that you can share with others in your network.

Players logging on from other computers will find this port showing up in their Multiplayer menu and can simply select it to join.

> **NOTE**   All players must have their own account to play on a LAN, and must be part of the same network.

SETTING UP A SMALL HOME SERVER

You can also host a server on a computer in your home and make it open to whomever you choose to invite. We have a friend who travels a lot for work, and he set up a server so that he could still play with his kids when he was out of town. You can download the Multiplayer Server executable file from the Mojang website (**Figure 8.6**).

Multiplayer Server

If you're running on Windows and just want to set up a server easily, download minecraft_server.1.6.4.exe and run it.

If you want to run the server on any other OS or without GUI it's a bit more involved (see this wiki article for a tutorial). First make sure you can use `java` from the command line. On Linux and Mac OS X this should already be set up but on Windows you might have to tinker with the PATH environment variable. Download and run minecraft_server.1.6.4.jar with `java -Xmx1024M -Xms1024M -jar minecraft_server.jar nogui`.

FIGURE 8.6   The Multiplayer Server download from Mojang

There are some complexities to setting up a server, so they are best set up by someone with a working knowledge of networking and configuring your system, network, and router. Different types of routers and their various configurations make this process more complex.

So if you want to host a server and do not have the knowledge yourself, find someone in your family or circle of friends that does know and ask them to help you. You can find good tutorials at http://minecraft.gamepedia.com/Tutorials/Setting_up_a_server. Make sure that whatever tutorial you use is up to date.

NOTE It is recommended that you host the server on a separate computer, rather than using the same one that players are using. Hosting a server can use a lot of resources on your computer, as can Minecraft itself.

SETTING UP A SMALL HOME SERVER ON WINDOWS

Windows is the easiest operating system to set up a home server on, and if you're looking to simply run a server in your house, you should find the steps straightforward.

1. Go to www.java.com/en/download/installed.jsp. This site will check that you have the latest version of Java, and if you don't, it will walk you through downloading and updating.

   After verifying your Java version, it is time to set up Minecraft.

2. Create a new folder named **Minecraft Server**.

3. Go to http://minecraft.net/download and download the most recent minecraft_server.exe file under Multiplayer Server. Put it in your new Minecraft Server folder.

4. Double-click the server.exe file. A new window opens (**Figure 8.7**). It will take a minute as it generates the new world. When the screen on the right says "Done," it is complete.

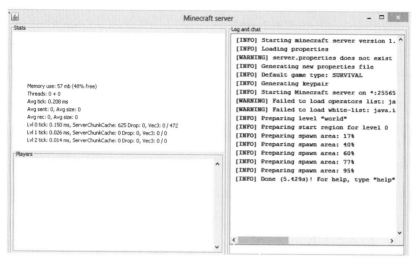

FIGURE 8.7 The Minecraft Server download window is the same on Windows and Mac.

SETTING UP A SMALL HOME SERVER ON MAC

Setting up a server on a Mac is a more involved process than on Windows. You can find a good tutorial at http://minecraft.gamepedia.com/Setting_up_a_server, and a search will turn up several others. Be sure that the tutorial you are following is up to date.

If you are comfortable with entering a bit of code, however, follow these steps carefully to set up a server.

1. Go to https://minecraft.net/download, download the current minecraft_server.jar file for Mac OS X, and place it on your desktop. There is a line of code that you will need later, so keep this page open.

2. Create a new folder on your desktop named **Minecraft Server**. Drag the minecraft_server.jar file that you just downloaded into this folder.

   Next, you need to create a start-up command so you can start your server.

3. In the Spotlight search field, type **text** to find TextEdit. Open TextEdit, and make sure it is in Plain Text mode (you'll find this setting under Format).

4. Enter the following code, as found at the tutorial at http:// minecraft.gamepedia.com/Setting_up_a_server. It will be easiest to simply cut and paste it from the tutorial (**Figure 8.8**).

```
#!/bin/bash

Cd "$(dirname "$0")"

exec java –Xmx1G –Xms1G  -jar minecraft_server.jar
```

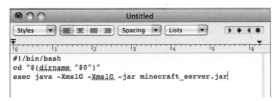

FIGURE 8.8 Setting up a server on Mac requires you to copy a bit of code.

This will provide your server with 1 GB of RAM. The amount can be changed in the bottom line of the code by changing the number in Xmx1G –Xms1G; for instance, Xms2G – Xms2G (G stands for gigabyte here), which will change the amount of allotted RAM to 2 GB, but you must make the same change to both parts.

5. Save this new file in the Minecraft Server folder you created, and name it **start.command**.

6. In the Spotlight search field, type **terminal** to find your Terminal. You can also find it in /Applications/Utilities/Terminal. Double-click it to open it.

7. Type in **chmod x+a** with a space after it.

8. Drag the start.command file from your Minecraft server into Terminal and press Enter. Close Terminal.

9. Double-click the start.commmand file in your Minecraft Server folder to start the server (**Figure 8.9**). A new window opens (Figure 8.7). It will take a minute as it generates the new world. When the screen on the right says "Done," it is complete. A series of folders will appear in your Minecraft Server folder.

FIGURE 8.9 Double-click the start file to start your server.

CONFIGURING YOUR WINDOWS OR MAC SERVER

Accessing the folders and configuring your server is the same for both Windows and Mac. To change the configurations, you need to stop the Minecraft server, which remains running on the server until you stop it.

1. Type **stop** into the box at the bottom of the Minecraft Server window (**Figure 8.10**). This will stop the server from running, which you will need to do to change some of the configurations in the server files before proceeding.

2. Open your Minecraft Server folder. You'll see that it has new files (**Figure 8.11**). One of these is your actual server launcher, and it is labeled minecraft_server.1.*.* (for the version of Minecraft you're running).

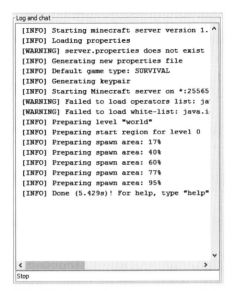

Log and chat

```
[INFO] Starting minecraft server version 1.
[INFO] Loading properties
[WARNING] server.properties does not exist
[INFO] Generating new properties file
[INFO] Default game type: SURVIVAL
[INFO] Generating keypair
[INFO] Starting Minecraft server on *:25565
[WARNING] Failed to load operators list: ja
[WARNING] Failed to load white-list: java.i
[INFO] Preparing level "world"
[INFO] Preparing start region for level 0
[INFO] Preparing spawn area: 17%
[INFO] Preparing spawn area: 40%
[INFO] Preparing spawn area: 60%
[INFO] Preparing spawn area: 77%
[INFO] Preparing spawn area: 95%
[INFO] Done (5.429s)! For help, type "help"
```

Stop

FIGURE 8.10 Typing "stop" in the lower-right screen will stop the server so you can make changes to the configurations. While this figure shows the Windows screen, this is the same on both Windows and Mac.

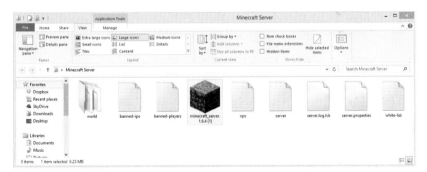

FIGURE 8.11 The Minecraft_server.exe will create several files.

3. Configure your new server with the following folder and file modifications:

- **world:** This is the world file created when your server started. It can be renamed or deleted to create a new world.

- **banned-ips** and **banned-players:** If you should need to ban someone by either their username or their IP, this is where you will enter the information. Double-click the file to open it, enter the names or IPs of the banned players in a list, placing each name on a new line, and close the file.

- **ops:** This is the operator file. You'll need to add your username so that you have operator powers on your server. Double-click the file, add your username and that of anyone else you'd like to give operator permissions to, and then close the file. You'll get a pop-up message asking if you want to save the changes. Click Yes.

- **server:** This is the server log; you can ignore it.

- **server.properties:** This is where all the specific properties of your server are stored. If you want to change them, you can find the information to do so on the Minecraft wiki page at http://minecraft.gamepedia.com/Server.properties.

- **white-list:** If you are planning to run an invitation-only server, this is where you will enter the players' names, placing each name on a new line. Double-click the file to open it, enter the names or IPs of the players in a list format, and close the file.

Your server will now be ready for use within your home.

PLAYING MINECRAFT FROM THE HOSTING SERVER

You can play Minecraft on the computer that is hosting the server, but this will likely slow down your game and can cause your server to lag and even close, depending on your computer. If possible, host your server from a different computer than the one you'll be playing on.

1. Open Minecraft, click Multiplayer, and then click Direct Connect.

2. In the Server Address field, type **localhost** (**Figure 8.12**).

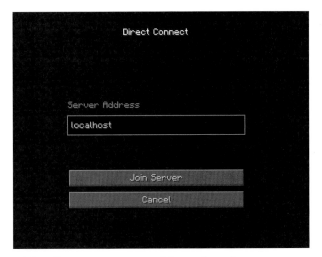

FIGURE 8.12 You can connect to Minecraft on the same computer you are hosting it on by typing "localhost" in the Server Address field.

PLAYING MINECRAFT ON A COMPUTER WITHIN YOUR WINDOWS HOME NETWORK

Players on other computers in your home network can connect using your router's internal IP address. For this, you will need your computer's internal IP address, or IPv4.

1. Open the command window by pressing Windows key+R. Enter **cmd (Figure 8.13)**.

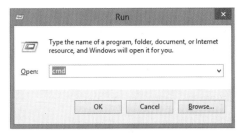

FIGURE 8.13 Use the command window to find your computer's internal IP address for sharing within your network.

2. Type **ipconfig** at the command prompt, and press Enter. The value for the IPv4 address is your internal IP.

3. To join from a computer that is not the host computer, open Minecraft, click Multiplayer, click Add Server, and enter the IPv4 address in the empty Server field. Click Done and you will be taken to your server list, where you can select the server and start playing.

PLAYING MINECRAFT ON A COMPUTER OUTSIDE YOUR NETWORK

To share your server with players outside your network, you need to open a port to your router. For this, you will need your hosting computer's external IP address.

1. Go to www.whatsmyip.org on the hosting computer to find your IP address. Your address displays. This will be the IP address that other players need to play on your home network.

   You need to use this IP address to open your port to the outside. This will take several steps, and is dependent on your router.

2. Go to http://portforward.com and following the directions there, or follow the directions on the Minecraft wiki page at http://minecraft. gamepedia.com/Setting_up_a_server#Configuring_the_ Minecraft_server.

   This is the trickiest step in the process, due to the wide range of routers and the multiple steps involved. If you have any difficulties or are seeking more information, it is best to go to the wiki page or do a search online for a tutorial. Be sure that it is for the most up-to-date version of Minecraft.

TROUBLESHOOTING YOUR SERVER SETUP

For people with basic computer skills, setting up a server can be frustrating because so many things can go wrong, from confusion with port forwarding to complications caused in configuration or by firewalls. Also, Mojang is continually upgrading and changing Minecraft, so some of these steps may change.

For up-to-date information, troubleshooting, and help, refer to the tutorial at http://minecraft.gamepedia.com/Setting_up_a_server. If your questions are not answered there, search the forums at http://www.minecraftforum.net/forum/152-server-support; if you don't find an answer to your specific question, post a question there. People in the Minecraft community are usually very willing to help.

MINECRAFT SERVER HOSTS

An alternative to setting up your own server is to use a Minecraft Server host. These sites, which typically charge a monthly fee, can be used to host a server and are often simpler to use and less resource-heavy than installing and hosting your own. An online search for hosts will result in plenty of options, offering a variety of services for a wide range of costs. There are reviews of different server hosts as well, allowing you to make an informed decision as to which host might best suit your specific needs.

PUBLIC SERVERS

Public servers, exactly as the name suggests, are servers hosted for the general public. Some are selective about who plays; others welcome everyone. There are definitely servers which are not family friendly, particularly for younger players.

Like many of you, I believed that my child would never play with others online, especially not at the age of 11, but after he had been playing single-player for a long while, and after he and I did a lot of research, I agreed to let him give it a try under my close supervision. It was a success, and we've never looked back.

I'm going to assume that the same will occur for the majority of readers, even those who are determined that their kids will stay off the Internet. And that's a good thing, because playing online offers the opportunity to build connections to others, learn the responsibilities that come with playing as part of a community, and learn and be inspired by fellow players.

 ## Wrednax

PLAYING WITH MY MOM on servers can be great, but sometimes it can cause trouble. Here are some of the best parts, and the issues.

Pros:

- You have someone in the house to talk to about what's going on with the server.
- You have someone on the server you can trust.
- You have someone to keep you on your toes so you don't say anything stupid.

Cons:

- Parents tend to have more knowledge and experience dealing with problems, so they tend to be more popular with the staff.
- Since a parent is on the server, a kid might not feel as comfortable taking on a villain role on a PVP server.

SERVERS AND COMMUNITY

The key component to playing on any server, regardless of the game, is that it pulls gaming out of the solo sphere and into the dynamics of social interactions. So many of the arguments about video games revolve around them being socially isolating, that players lose their ability to interact with others. Gaming has changed drastically in recent years, and the social aspect is one of the areas of greatest growth. From multiplayer role-playing games to Minecraft servers that allow players to work together or play against one another, there are endless ways for gamers to play together.

As with anything, there are of course positive and negative aspects. Some people hide behind the anonymity of a screen and username to bully, but others use that anonymity to show more of their true selves than they might in real life—the less guarded, more caring side of themselves—because they don't face peer pressure to be who they are not. I know gamers whose friends at school have no idea that they play, let alone that they stream live videos every night. Gaming can still carry a stigma. Gamers are seen as geeky, and they often wish to hide those aspects of themselves. On servers, they find acceptance to be who they truly are.

Playing on servers changes the gameplay, because they provide something a computer program, no matter how complex, cannot. Other players bring in the randomness of personal choice and of human nature in all its glorious unpredictability. Social connections—and social divides—form. Goals are set, and people work together for common good or against each other in competition. This leads to more engaging gameplay. The amount of learning that occurs may surprise you.

Players need to communicate with each other, make plans, and set goals. They must divide tasks, share labor, and negotiate and manage shared space and resources. Even on combat-focused servers, players often work in teams. They learn to persevere and to support their weakest players in order to advance. They must learn to plan ahead, take advantage of opportunities, and be spontaneous. They have to learn that being defeated is OK and not to attack the weak in their group, because next time that weak link might be the strongest.

Online gaming allows for roleplaying, for exploring who you are and who you want to be. It lets players shine and allows them to safely explore risk-taking. They learn to forge alliances and discover what betrayal might feel like. There are countless lessons to be learned through games, if only we stop for a moment and realize that there is a lot more going on than an avatar swinging a sword.

TYPES OF SERVERS

There are hundreds of Minecraft servers to play on. Creative servers are basically creative worlds with all the same properties as on a single-player server. There are survival servers. PVP servers are common—they use a variety of mods and plugins, depending on the type of gameplay they are promoting. Some servers are "factions" servers, with a specific type of plugin that allows players to gain or lose land for their side based on deaths and kills. Other PVP servers use Towny plugins to create towns in which only members can build.

Build servers are where players might build on a survival map, much like playing a single-player game that requires collecting of resources. Player-to-player combat is often turned off on these servers.

Themed servers might include a roleplay aspect, or they might have a specific build style or general theme. Adventure maps have restricted building, often focusing instead on an end goal and a more standard video game experience that's set in a Minecraft world. Some plugins, like Tekkit or Feed the Beast, have added advanced technology, with complex machines that can be built.

Given the wide range of servers available, there is certain to be one that suits every player, from small, community-based servers to massive roleplaying or PVP servers that host thousands of players.

FINDING A SERVER

There are many ways to find servers to play on. An online search is a good place to start. Often the search result pages include reviews, comments, and votes by players, as well as descriptions of what they offer. If you're looking for something specific, such as "family friendly," include that in your search.

Checking blogs and vlogs is another way to find servers, and again a search will get you on the right track. Friends and colleagues whose kids play are an often-overlooked resource.

Once you find a server you might be interested in, you can search for it by name. Not all lists update regularly or provide the same information. Cross-referencing is not a bad thing.

ADDING AND SAVING A SERVER

It's easy to join a new server, and Minecraft will save the information so you can return easily.

1. On the Minecraft main menu page, click Multiplayer. You will be at the Multiplayer menu (Figure 8.1).

2. Click Add Server. You will be taken to the Edit Server Info page, which is where you add new servers and edit servers currently in your list (**Figure 8.14**).

FIGURE 8.14 To add a server, simply enter the server address into the Server Address field and click Done.

3. In the Server Name field, enter a name or description of your choosing.

4. In the Server Address field, enter the IP or other address for the server you wish to add.

5. Click Done, and you will be returned to the Play Multiplayer page, where you will see your newly added server in the list.

6. To join a server, click it in the list of servers to highlight it. Click the Join Server button and you'll be connected to the server.

PLAYING BY THE RULES

It is important to respect the server's rules, or you may find yourself temporarily kicked off (**Figure 8.15**), put into a server jail (yes, some servers have a jail plugin), or even banned. Server staff monitor your behavior and track who has been banned. Many have methods to appeal bans as well. Servers often have forums on which the rules are listed, and most have the rules posted at a central spawn point when you first log on. Here are some common guidelines:

■ **Staffing.** Servers are usually staffed by volunteer players or server hosts. Staff are ranked, with *mods*, or moderators, at the lowest level (this can be confusing to new players, as game plugins and modifications are also called mods). Operators (ops) have more technical abilities and access, and administrators (admins) have full access and typically keep the server running. There is often an owner, who may or may not play.

On some servers, players who donate money can become staff; on others, staff are selected based on experience, time on the server, or merit. Some staff take their roles very seriously, and others not so much. One thing to watch for when selecting a server is the culture—from the staff on down through the players.

FIGURE 8.15 If you are kicked off a server, you often get a message stating the reason, such as when Rawcritics staff member Sprollucy jokingly kicked me off to go work on this book.

- **Anti-griefing.** *Griefing* is when you deliberately destroy something on the server. Although a very few servers turn a blind eye to griefing, most take it quite seriously. This is to protect players who worked hard on a build and don't want to see their work ruined. Some servers have mods and plugins that protect work and allow for plots of land on which only specific players may place or remove blocks. Others use world-guard mods to protect builds. Even in these cases, trying to break blocks may be enough to alert staff and get a player kicked off a server.

- **Behavior and language.** Servers usually have rules about language in chat and about actions toward other players. Some servers, particularly family-friendly ones, have zero tolerance for rude or inappropriate language, while others are much more lenient. Some staff simply mute players who are being inappropriate as a first warning; others take more direct steps.

- **Mod restrictions.** Most servers have rules about what modifications you can use. They try to limit cheating by allowing or disallowing specific mods. You can be kicked off or banned from a server for using illegal mods. For example, on Rawcritics there is an instant ban for the use of an XRay mod, which allows you to see diamonds and other ores underground. Staff on all servers have tools that allow them to monitor and decide if an illegal mod has been used.

Take the time to read a server's rules. You may be asked to take a quiz, or to sign an agreement that you will follow the rules. There may be tasks you need to do, or you may need to wait a given period of time before you are allowed to build or explore. Each server has its own rules and guidelines—it makes sense to abide by them.

ONLINE SAFETY

In Chapter 3, we looked at guidelines for being safe online. Playing on servers is a big part of stepping outside the safe confines of your home, and for younger children, single-player games or games on a limited-access home server are the best bet. It is too hard to control what they will have access to, and they are not yet mature enough to know what to do or say in situations that might be frustrating or even scary for them. Xander was allowed to try a server at age 11, and that felt young to me, but I knew how mature he was and I was right there. And the players on the server were for the most part extremely welcoming and friendly. Even so, there were times when he needed help to sort things out, or to know how to best respond to a situation. Being aware of your child's personality and their maturity level will help you know when they might be ready to play online. As your kids get older, and if they are showing responsibility, you will be able to relax your guidelines. In the meantime, I think that there is little reason for kids under 11 or 12 to be playing on public servers, unless they are closely supervised or on a family-specific server.

The other pointers from Chapter 3 include keeping communication open, working with mutual trust and respect, and knowing where your

kids are spending their time online. If you have open, clear communication with your kids, you'll know where they are playing and what
they're doing. Trusting them to be safe and make responsible choices
will actually encourage them to do so.

But what about the questions we all wonder about—just who are
our children meeting online? What about online predators? The fact is
that there are people who go online to seek out vulnerable youth. And
they are clever, they disguise themselves, and they look for those who
are lonely or at risk. At the same time, there are a lot of myths about
the prevalence of sexual predators.

Many studies have been done about online safety, and the manner
in which the information is interpreted and presented can vary greatly.
Look at the research yourself, make up your own mind about it, and
use that information along with your personal and family beliefs to
establish rules for your family.

Children are more educated about online safety than ever before.
It is important to talk regularly about hard issues like identity, sexuality, self-esteem, and common sense. All these issues factor in to
how vulnerable your child is and how they portray themselves online.
Simply relying on parental control programs and telling children not to
give out personal information is not enough. Younger kids, the ones we
worry about, are generally pretty safe online. They might stumble on
to something they shouldn't, but parents are vigilant when their kids
are younger. It is as they enter their teens and beyond that they face
greater risks.

You need to know how your kids are presenting themselves. This is
vitally important. Adolescence in particular is an amazingly hard time
for most kids. They can start to question themselves, their value, and
their worth. They can develop vulnerabilities that make them suscep-
tible to lies and stories. They might fall for a romantic story or be more
easily wooed. However, they also get clever about creating personas
that are not who they are in real life. The anonymity of the Internet
allows them the flexibility to roleplay and take greater risks. Knowing your teen—what they are insecure about, what pressures they are

facing, and what they are worried about—is important to keeping them safe online.

Help them find their inner resources. Remind them that they don't need to pretend to be someone else to be loved. Give them enough freedom that they can take risks in a safe manner. Show them respect and trust—it needs to be earned, but let them impress you with what they can do rather than constantly expecting them to let you down. They will rise to the occasion, and they'll be stronger and more resilient for it.

Rather than lecturing them or listing rules, have them tell you what they are doing to protect themselves. They might surprise you with their wisdom. Ask them to tell you their thoughts on online safety, and use these conversations to open further dialogue. Enlist their help in supporting their peers, who might be more vulnerable. Turn their knowledge into skills, and help them develop tools to be safe.

All of this has to be within your own family's boundaries. Practical rules—like the computer being in a public space, limiting Internet access to certain hours, or other guidelines—are individual to your family's needs and beliefs. Talk to other families to see what guidelines they use. Consistency among friends and families can make it easier for kids to follow rules.

ONLINE COMMUNICATION

One of the most important aspects of playing online is communicating with the people you're playing with. There are many ways to do this, from in-game chat or messaging to Skype.

MULTIPLAYER CHAT

Multiplayer servers have a system of chatting within the game. The chat scrolls up the screen, and you can follow and join the dialogue.

To join the chat, simply press the letter T on your keyboard; a bar appears at the bottom of your screen (**Figure 8.16**). If you miss something in chat, you can scroll back a short way with your mouse wheel or the Up Arrow key. Players can post links in chat, and if you need to copy or paste something, you can use the standard keyboard commands for these actions: Control+C to copy, Control+X to cut, and Control+V to paste. (On a Mac, use the Command key rather than the Control key.)

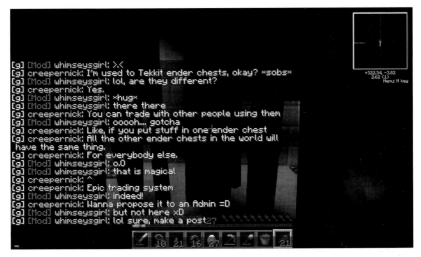

FIGURE 8.16 In multiplayer Minecraft, chat messages appear onscreen.

When you type your message, everyone on the server sees it. This is known as *global* chat. Many servers have different commands for speaking locally, chatting in specific channels, or sending a private message.

CHAT ETIQUETTE

Many servers have a code of conduct for chatting. Pay attention to what is being said in chat, and if in doubt, ask what the chat rules and guidelines are. Some servers do not tolerate swearing or inappropriate language, including sexual, racist, or demeaning talk. Bullying and put-downs may not be tolerated, especially on servers that say they are family friendly. Players might be temporarily kicked off the server or banned for things they say in chat. Other servers don't place any limits on content, and you might be shocked at the language and messages. Chat will give you an idea of the culture of a server. This is something to watch for and monitor when your child ventures onto a new server.

The following are some general chat rules:

■ The use of *caps*, or all capital letters (LIKE THIS), is typically frowned upon. It is seen as the written equivalent of shouting, and on some servers it is treated as seriously as inappropriate content.

■ *Spamming* is when a player repeats themselves over and over, or fills the chat with their content (such as taking a separate line for each word of a sentence). It too is frowned upon, as it can be very frustrating for the other players. Also, many servers don't allow advertising other servers or websites.

■ Say hi when you join a server, then observe the chat for a bit or join in. Some players may welcome you, but sometimes players are very quiet, especially if they're working on something or if that is the culture on that server. And if they have the plugins for more chat options, players may be engaged in smaller group conversations that will not show up in the global chat.

■ VOICE CHAT

Often players are invited to join a call, either with one other person or with a group. Skype is often used for this, as are group chatrooms through programs like Mumble or Teamspeak.

This worried me as a parent, not knowing who Xander was going to be talking with or the tone of the conversation. My view has changed, though it took some time and lots of discussion before I was comfortable with him being in calls. His first calls were with a homeschool friend in another town. Now, however, he and I often communicate via Skype when we're playing or even when we're working in different rooms. It's actually opened up dialogue between us. I use Skype both for messaging and for talking to friends from the server.

Calls are also handy when people are playing together and want an easy way to communicate about a build, a raid, or any other project. You don't need to stop to write, so you can just keep talking. Many chats use a feature called "push to talk," which is just as it sounds— you assign a button on your keyboard or mouse to be your "talk" button, and you must press it to be heard. Using this feature is considered good voice-chat etiquette, though in games where there is no time to push buttons, just leaving the call open is acceptable.

TYPES OF VOICE CHAT

Skype is a free program that allows you to make free voice or video calls or to chat using text. Calls can be between two people, or a group of people can hold a call. Web links can be shared via the chat window, and in a group call, individuals can send private chat messages to one another.

Mumble and TeamSpeak are alternatives to Skype that have been designed for group calls. They allow players to meet in chat rooms and converse with each other. But because they are much more open to random people coming and going (not just those you have invited), it can be a good idea to begin with Skype.

EQUIPMENT

Although you can chat without a headset (headphones and microphone combined in one unit), doing so can be challenging for both you and others in your call. Your computer's microphone might not be strong enough to capture your voice, or it might pick up all the sounds in room, like your typing or the sound of your hard drive engaging. And without headphones, your speakers will broadcast everything back through your microphone. At the very least, you need headphones for a call, and if you'll be using voice chat a lot, a good headset is a good idea.

Look online for reviews of headsets. Gaming headsets are designed to balance the game sounds with voice chat, and they're usually designed with maximum comfort in mind. Sets can be wireless or wired—there are advantages and disadvantages to both. Wireless headsets don't have issues with loose wires, and they allow for mobility, but their sound quality can be worse than that of wired headsets, and they need to be recharged or have their batteries replaced.

CALL SAFETY

You might want to set up specific rules for using Skype. If you don't want your children to be visible to others, you will need to make sure they know not to make video calls, or you will need to remove or disable your computer's webcam. Video calls do not need to be the default, and many players never use them.

SETTING UP A SKYPE ACCOUNT

To use Skype, you'll need to set up a user account. You might consider using the same username you or your kids have for Minecraft.

1. Go to skype.com. Click the Join button, and you will be taken to the Create an Account page (**Figure 8.17**).

2. Enter the information for your profile on this page, including your name and email address. Only the boxes with asterisks (*) are required—you can choose how much information goes into your profile or your child's. You are reminded by Skype that anyone on Skype can access your profile information. You can also edit this information from your account settings page once your account is set up.

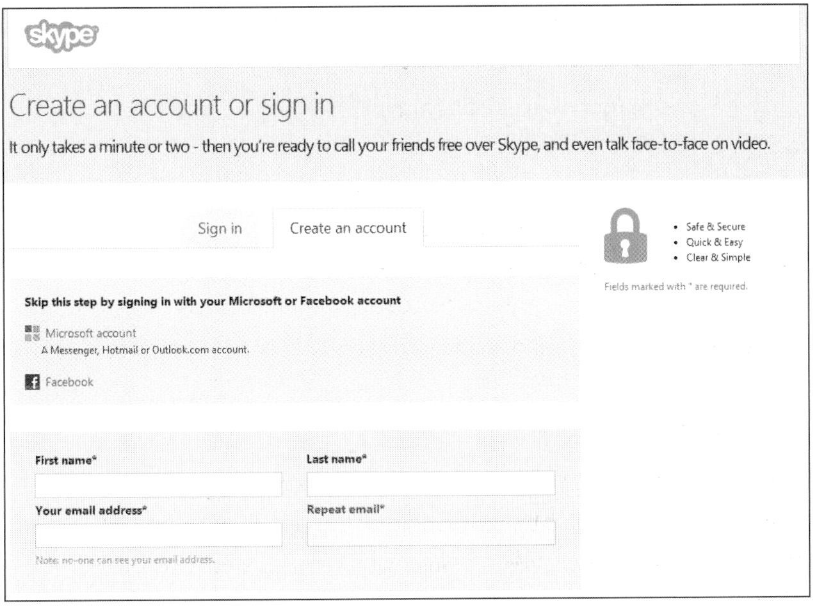

FIGURE 8.17 You can create an account or sign in to Skype at skype.com.

3. Enter your Skype name and password. For consistency, you might want to use your Minecraft username, but you should use a different password. Re-enter your password to verify it.

4. Enter the CAPTCHA (Completely Automated Public Turing Test to Tell Computers and Humans Apart) you see in the "Type the text above here*" field (**Figure 8.18** on the next page).

5. Take a look at the Skype Terms of Use and the Skype Privacy Statement links at the bottom of the page, then click the "I agree – Continue" button.

You will be taken to a welcome page, where you can download Skype if it isn't already loaded on your computer. You will then return to the welcome screen, where you can take a tour of Skype, edit your profile, or make your first call.

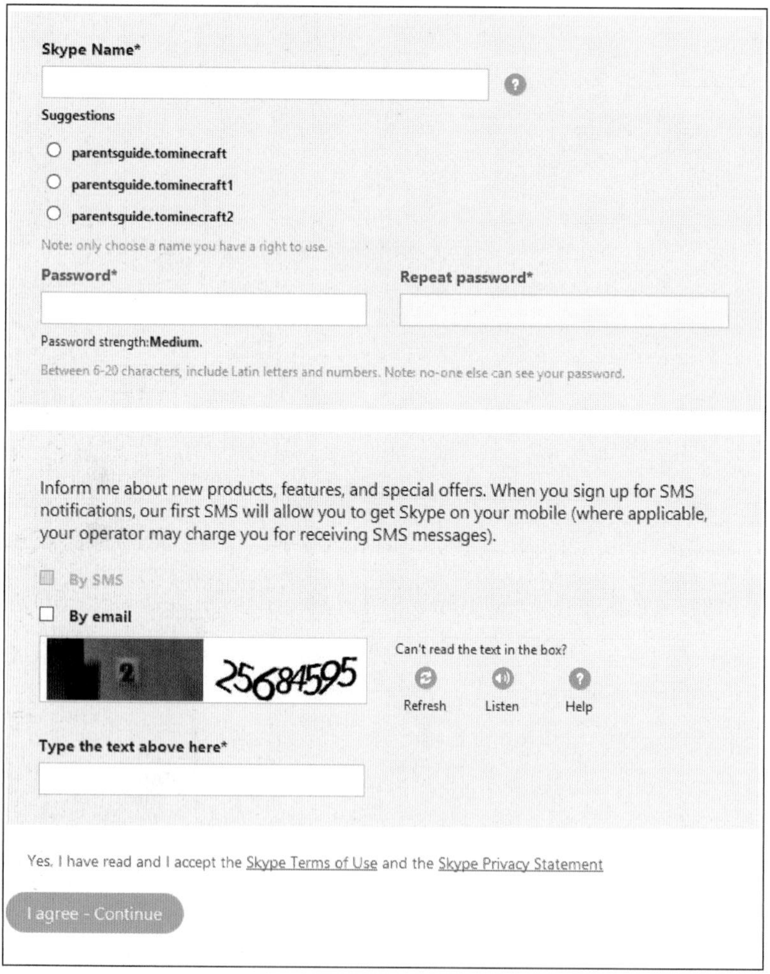

FIGURE 8.18 Select a unique username for your Skype account.

Playing and Chatting with Your Children

ALTHOUGH WE OCCASIONALLY have our ups and downs, I think gaming together has helped Xander and me stay connected. We share many of the same interests, and we have a similar quirky and often sarcastic sense of humor. We are also very different in a lot of ways, which is a good thing. Xander's love of history and science runs far deeper than mine, and Xander loves to take a leadership role, whereas I like to be in the background. Playing together has helped us grow closer, and we've had to work on communicating. We've made good discoveries about how to talk with each other and, more importantly, how to listen to each other.

On the server, the parent and child roles are gone. I respect Xander as another player, one who has been playing Minecraft much longer than I have and who was on the server first. We may disagree, but no more so than we do with other players. And we've had to weather his frustration over my being asked to be staff, something he has long wanted. That has been our biggest hurdle, but one that we've worked through.

Chatting via instant messaging on Skype really works for us. Over my years of working with teens, I've learned that face-to-face conversations seem to bring up defensive, reactionary responses. I've long recommended that parents try conversing while doing a side-by-side activity—doing the dishes or meal prep, for instance, or even riding in the car. And I've long been a proponent of using a notebook to communicate on important issues—write a note, leave the book for your child, and have them do the same. It allows a bit of space between you.

We've stumbled upon a new, modern-day version of this with our messaging. I know other families who communicate via email and texting as well. Somehow we are able to be more candid, to discuss the trickier stuff as well as the day-to-day little things where conflict could arise. Somehow that small bit of distance works wonders.

Playing and Chatting with Your Children *(continued)*

I strongly recommend playing with your kids. If you can't find common ground gaming, seek it elsewhere. But all the benefits of gaming I've discussed are good for adults too. Just because it is new doesn't mean you won't love it. And having your child be better than you at something— and teach you for a change—opens doors and teaches lessons about respect, patience, and what it feels like to be in the other person's shoes. It's worth exploring.

CHAPTER 9

SEE WHAT I MADE?

ONE OF THE BEST THINGS about Minecraft is the never-ending creative possibilities, all of which allow you to make just about anything you want. Whether you're working on your own or with others, you can create amazing builds, new types of automated farms or other machines, pieces of art, and so much more. Beyond this there are tips and techniques, building styles, and worlds that are too amazing to keep to yourself. And what is creation without an audience? This is where online sharing comes into play.

SHARING ONLINE

You have a variety of ways to share your work and ideas online, from blogs and vlogs to posting live video as you play. You can share openly, or you can share with a select group of viewers by invitation only, and the options for what and how to share are endless.

■ WHY SHARE ONLINE?

It's a very human trait to want to show off what we've created—to share knowledge and experiences and to provide tips to others. Minecraft encourages players to explore and create in ways that are very different from other games. And let's face it: Most of us take great satisfaction in sharing with others.

Minecraft is a digital game that's played on a computer (tablets and iPhones are still computers), so it makes sense to want to share it in that same medium. You can invite family or friends to watch over your shoulder and share in that manner, but sometimes the urge strikes you to share with a larger audience. YouTube, Twitch, and deviantArt can help you do that.

You and your children can experience Minecraft via YouTube and watch tutorials or accomplish specific tasks. You might watch "let's plays" to follow a player as they play, or you might watch music videos. This may encourage you or your children to create and post your own videos.

Sharing creations and content online does not require a server. Single-player worlds can make much more sense for sharing; since the work belongs to one player (the one who posted it), the logistics of sharing it is much simpler.

■ HOW TO SHARE ONLINE

You have lots of options for displaying your creations online, from creating videos for YouTube to posting pictures in a blog or sharing art on a visual art site such as deviantArt. Each of these requires you to capture your images in video or still images before you upload them. Although capturing video and pictures may seem like a daunting task, it's actually very easy.

YOUTUBE

According to YouTube, 100 hours of video content are loaded to it every minute, and 1 billion viewers watch every month. YouTube is the best-known place to find user-made videos on pretty much any subject. It's incredible how much material is out there, but what's handiest for new Minecraft users is that there are thousands of tutorials covering any aspect of the game you may be having difficulty with.

Some kids have spent a lot of time on YouTube and are familiar with all the current *memes*—current, trending ideas that are often humorous and that spread across the Internet like wildfire. Nyan Cat—the animated, pixelated cathead on a Pop Tart body that sails through a night sky trailing a rainbow to a catchy but repetitive tune—is a long-standing meme. Kids might watch their favorite shows on YouTube and might already have favorite vloggers that they watch. Others might be new to the idea of watching videos online, due to family rules or a lack of time spent exploring online or even for technological reasons such as an older computer or slow Internet speeds.

Although YouTube has some basic guidelines and rules about what can be posted, it still has a lot of content that would be considered adult. For this reason, it is important to monitor what your child is watching and ensure that it fits within your family bounds. As kids get older, it can be possible to let them make their own decisions about what they watch, but this is dependent on the child and still bears monitoring. Keeping communication open and conversing about topics such as sexuality, exploitation, and safety is important, not just in regard to YouTube content but to life in general.

YouTube allows you to make playlists, make channels on which to save videos you've watched, and follow or subscribe to users so that their new videos appear on your page automatically without you having to search for them. You can also upload your own videos to your channel; once you've done so, you can choose to keep the videos private, share them with people you select, or make them available to the public. YouTube also allows you to track how many people view your videos, and you can rate, share, and comment on other videos; viewers can do the same with yours if you have shared them publicly. The creator can leave information about the video, provide links, or simply comment on the video, all of which is easy and accomplished with simple editing tools. The quality of videos on YouTube ranges from unpolished, simple films to complex, professional-quality videos. And as you might expect with something that is wide open and available to all, when it comes to YouTube almost anything goes.

Videos can be made with any digital video camera, including the camera on your phone, the webcam on your computer, or a high-end video camera. There are also programs, like Fraps and Bandicam, that allow you to record what is on your computer screen or broadcast it live. Editing programs abound, including Windows Movie Maker, Adobe Premiere Pro, and one within YouTube itself.

LIVESTREAMING

Livestreaming is a method of delivering video dynamically by broadcasting what is happening on your screen live to viewers. Livestreams of gaming are very popular and are hosted on many sites. Twitch.tv and Stream.tv are two popular examples of livestream sites for gamers.

When livestreaming, the player typically talks while playing, and more often than not appears in an inset screen in the corner of the viewing area. Viewers can chat with each other, and the livestreamer can read the chat comments as they appear, responding dynamically if they wish. Viewers can subscribe to players and sign up for email or text notifications when players they are following start a new stream.

Because livestreams are truly live and not edited, they can be harder to monitor for content. Some streamers are more family friendly. Many streamers have rules for etiquette, and some have moderators who help keep things more or less on track.

Livestreamers may have guests join them via programs such as Skype. Some link up and play together with split screens so viewers can follow the conversation between players and view the screens of all the participants. The real-time interaction between gamer and viewer and between viewers makes livestreaming a very different experience than watching videos on YouTube.

SHARING ART AND TEXT

For those who prefer to write or post pictures rather than create videos, there are many blog-hosting sites. These sites allow you to upload pictures and write about what you've been creating, create a tutorial, or share your work directly. These sites can be private, invitation only, or public. People also post on forums (more about these in Chapter 10) or create personal websites; others stick to social media sites like Facebook. It really depends on what your goal is: to share with friends and family or to reach a much larger audience. Your interest and technical ability in hosting a webpage or using a program like WordPress to create a blog can influence how you present yourself online and by extension how you support your child in doing so.

Websites like deviantArt are aimed at visual artists, and Minecraft-inspired art has found its way there too, though most is digital or drawn art rather than actual project builds or creations. Wiki pages such as Minecraft Creations allow players to upload pictures or screenshots of their creations. Reddit is another place for posting images.

Like YouTube and livestreaming sites, most of these options can be set up to invite feedback from viewers or guests who come to see your work, and some dialogue may happen should you wish to respond.

■ WHAT TO SHARE

Pretty much anything goes when it comes to sharing creations or discussing Minecraft, but most things fall into the following categories:

tutorials; walkthroughs; vlogs; movies and music videos; and mods, skins, and texture packs.

TUTORIALS

Tutorials are the how-tos, the directions on everything from getting started and surviving your first night to redstone designs for simple machines or directions for massive builds.

Creating a tutorial requires some forethought in order to present the information in a clear manner that viewers or followers will be able to replicate. If careful thought isn't put into the process, there can be much frustration. Minecraft changes (sometimes drastically) from update to update, so tutorials can become outdated overnight. Read the comments on the tutorial see if you have found an up-to-date tutorial that others have found useful.

If you or your child want to try your hand at creating a tutorial, it helps to watch others first to see what works and what doesn't. Again, it is important to make sure the steps are clear and in sequence, and that you don't assume the viewer has knowledge of anything beyond the basics (and if it is aimed at first-time Minecraft players, you can't even assume that much).

WALKTHROUGHS, LET'S PLAYS, AND MORE

Walkthroughs and let's plays can be text (as in a blog) or pre-recorded or live video. Walkthroughs and let's plays are similar. In both, the gamer is playing through a game and providing a commentary. A let's play is less focused and often seems completely aimless, yet they can be very entertaining (perhaps because of that very randomness). Walkthroughs, however, are more planned and deliberate and seem to be focused on surviving the first night or learning how to navigate the game, and they're much more like guided tutorials.

There are many entertaining and popular Minecraft let's plays. Some have millions of subscribers, like the Yogscast (two players who tend to bumble their way through entertaining escapades) and

Mindcrack (25 players who have individual channels and play together in various combinations). Some let's plays and walkthroughs are very family friendly, and others are not, if only for the occasional slip of a swearword.

It's fun to watch players explore and build, mine and create, and run into the same frustrations as anyone else, even if they've had tons of experience and are incredibly knowledgeable. Some are very private and focus only on the game, while others are more open and use their let's plays as a vlog, talking about whatever comes to mind. Many play lots of other games, which can be a good way to explore unfamiliar games your kids talk about.

Some videos are simply tours of builds. They aren't tutorials that explain how to make something; they just show the work, the design, and the build elements. Sometimes there is a commentary, and other times they are simply set to music.

VLOGS

Vlogs simply feature the vlogger in front of a camera. There are fewer Minecraft vlogs, but some vloggers can be found reviewing the game, talking about updates, or discussing other Minecraft-related information.

MOVIES AND MUSIC VIDEOS

Minecraft fans have turned the game into an art form. Using 3D animation tools, they make detailed, scripted movies and music videos (**Figure 9.1**).

These movies require a lot of time and hard work. Animating the characters, a process known as rendering, takes time and skill. Writing a script, rendering the animation, editing, and adding sound and possibly voice tracks are big jobs that require skill, knowledge, and practice. Using the same process to make a music video for an original Minecraft song also takes drive, skill, and knowledge. The shows and videos are entertaining, but they are also awe-inspiring because of the amount of time and energy that has gone into them.

The fact that many of these, including the image in Figure 9.1, are made by high school students—and that they are self-taught or have learned from their peers—is utterly inspiring to me. And not just to me—these teens are inspiring others around them.

FIGURE 9.1 A scene from an animated trailer created by Nurb

MODS, SKINS, AND TEXTURE PACKS

Mods can be added to a basic, or *vanilla*, Minecraft game to add elements or change how the game is played. Skins are what give your character its appearance in the game; they can be created using a number of programs, and prefabricated skins can be found online. *Texture packs* are almost like skins for the individual blocks—they change the appearance of the blocks in the game, so a player can have blocks that suit the theme and setting of the build.

Skins can be posted on sites like minecraftskins.com, and texture packs and mods can be found on sites such as minecraftforum.net. The creators of these programs typically do it not for money but out of a love for the game and a desire to add new layers to the gameplay.

■ SAFELY SHARING

We've already discussed online safety, but posting online adds a new layer of difficulty. You must have a sense of what your children are putting out there. Communication is key, as is being open and willing to support your child. If you aren't, they won't stop—they'll just keep it a secret from you.

I can personally attest to this, as I know I number of players who stream and post videos regularly, and their parents have no idea what they are doing. They fear that their parents won't understand, will use their interest to control them, or will stop them entirely. And the worst part is that these teens do amazing work, their livestreams and videos are fantastic, and they are passionate about and dedicated to what they do.

It comes back to paying attention, being genuinely interested, and being open to teen culture. Chances are that there will be swearing or what we would consider inappropriate content in their streams. But among their peers, it is not so inappropriate, so long as it isn't too extreme and is contained to times with friends. I don't encourage or condone this, but I do understand that it happens. If it stays at a reasonable level and doesn't come out in inappropriate places, such as Grandma's, it's not nearly as bad as many believe.

Kids must be on their guard so they don't accidentally give away information in a chat or conversation. It can be easy for them to slip up when they're joking with friends in a stream. Maybe they use a given name instead of a username, or give other personal information. In a video, it can be edited out; in a livestream, not so much. In these situations, it's best not to draw attention to a slip. It could very well be that no one notices, and the chances that it would be revealing enough to cause any issues are very small. Likewise, the odds are small that someone is watching a stream or video with the intent to harm.

CREATING A YOUTUBE CHANNEL

Having a YouTube channel is the same thing as having an account or page. Having a channel allows you to create playlists, save videos to watch later, subscribe to other channels, follow specific people, and upload and share your own videos.

It's not a bad idea to set up a channel for each person in your family who uses YouTube. Xander started out using mine, and now disentangling the two is a monumental task.

1. Go to YouTube.com. Click the Sign In button in the upper-right corner. You are redirected to the sign-in page (**Figure 9.2**).

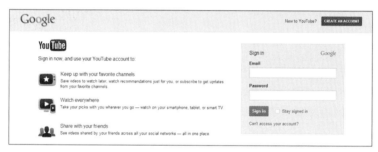

FIGURE 9.2 The YouTube sign-in page.

YouTube is owned by Google, so you will need a Google account in order to sign in. If you don't have a Google account, follow steps 2–8 to create one.

Otherwise, simply enter your email address and password, and then click the Sign In button to go to the YouTube welcome page. Skip to step 9.

2. To create a Google account, click the Create an Account button in the upper-right corner. You are taken to a registration screen (**Figure 9.3**).

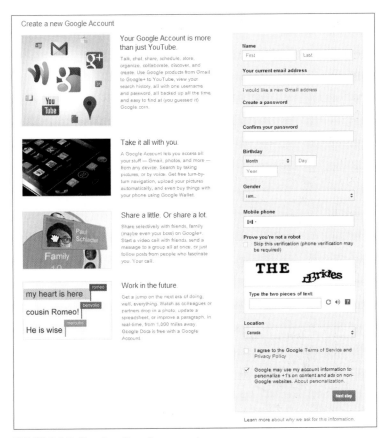

FIGURE 9.3 Create a Google account.

3. Enter your email address. You can choose to use an existing email address, or you can create a new Gmail account. If you decide to create a new account, you can try the same username as you have for your Mojang account or use something different. Have several names in mind in case your first choice is taken.

4. Select the Terms and Services check box. If you do not want Google to personalize your account with Google+, deselect that box.

5. Enter a phone number. This is used to verify your account after you complete this page, either through a text or a voice call.

6. Click Next Step. You will receive a code, either by text or voice.

7. Enter the code you received in the "Enter verification code" field, and click Next. You are taken to a profile page, where you can add a picture.

8. Click Back to YouTube at the bottom of the page. You are taken to the main YouTube page.

9. Watch some videos, and take a bit of time to get to know the various features, such as the Watch Later option and subscribing to other channels.

◼ DOCUMENTING YOUR ACCOMPLISHMENTS

This is a topic that could easily fill an entire book. Here are some of the basics so you can capture your children's work when there are images they want to keep.

TAKING SCREENSHOTS

Screenshots (or *screenies*, as they are often called) are pictures of your entire screen. In Minecraft, it is very easy to take screenshots, and it is the easiest way to capture images. Just press F2 on Windows, or Fn+F2 on a Mac.

The images are stored as PNG files in a Minecraft screenshots folder, using the date and time as the filename. On Windows, this folder is located at %appdata%\.minecraft\screenshots; on a Mac, it can be found at ~/Library/Application Support/minecraft/screenshots.

TAILORING WHAT YOU SEE ON THE SCREEN

To clear the screen of your chat, inventory, and arm so it shows only what your character is facing, press F1; press F1 again to return the screen to the normal view. Press F3 to see all your data, including your coordinates; this is an easy way to document your location.

CAPTURING VIDEO

There are many free programs that you can download to record Mine-craft video. Fraps and Bandicam are a couple of the most popular for Windows. On the Mac, you can use QuickTime, which is already installed.

These programs, like Minecraft itself, change and update regu-larly, and new ones come out frequently. Search online for "Minecraft video capture software" to discover what people are currently using and recommending. You can post your videos as they are, without edit-ing, or you can look for online tutorials on video editing. The tools that come with YouTube are fairly basic, but they might be all you need.

UPLOADING VIDEO

Uploading a video to YouTube is straightforward. On the main YouTube page, click Upload. You'll then see the screen in **Figure 9.4**.

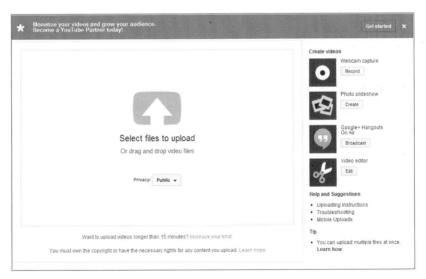

FIGURE 9.4 Youtube's video upload page.

As you can see, you can upload a video by clicking the large arrow in the center of the screen. You can also set your privacy settings, and you can set simple options to film with your webcam, make a slide-show, broadcast live, or edit a saved video. The menu on the bottom right links to uploading instructions, troubleshooting tips, and directions for uploading from a mobile device. Because links and sites change quickly, it is best to refer to YouTube for up-to-date directions.

LIVESTREAMING

Livestreaming is a little more complex and involved than recording and posting videos, but many 13-year-olds are able to do it. There are many steps to get started, but once you have registered with a site such as Twitch or Ustream (**Figure 9.5**), you'll find directions and tutorials that walk you through configuring your system, selecting the proper video capture program, setting up Flash Player, and broadcasting the stream itself.

Before you consider streaming, spend some time watching streams and seeing what your kids are interested in. At the very least, you'll be able to understand them when they talk about streaming.

FIGURE 9.5 Twitch is an excellent place to watch players, such as Sprollucy, livestream, as well as to try it yourself.

CHAPTER 10

THE BIGGER PICTURE

THE SOCIETAL CHANGES that are happening around technology are steamrolling as people connect through not just personal computers but also smartphones and tablets. And Minecraft has expanded in many directions, from social connections to educational applications to creative projects.

COMMUNITY

Minecraft has brought together people of all ages and walks of life. It's a common ground that allows people to share their interests and work together in online Minecraft communities.

There are hundreds of online Minecraft communities to choose from. Players of all ages have formed supportive communities in which they share game ideas, ask for information or advice, and discuss art, video, and music. There is something out there for everyone—from groups that are family focused or educational to those that are purely about gaming.

■ FORUMS

One main way that online communities gather is through forums. *Forums* are a type of website organized in a way that allows members to share text-based conversations. Topics are listed in a menu, under headings that fit the community (**Figure 10.1**). Conversations that spring up are known as *threads*, and members can write (or in forum lingo, post) in those threads. The responses are listed sequentially, and a thread can end up being hundreds of pages long, though most are much shorter. Forum members can answer previous responses directly, quote others, and post pictures, Internet links, and videos.

Staff (often volunteers) moderate forums to ensure that guidelines and rules (which are usually clearly posted) are followed. Distinct communities and cultures tend to form within individual forums. Some are purely informative (where, for example, people might seek advice on computer hardware), and others can be more collaborative and mutually supportive, such as a forum for those with a specific medical condition.

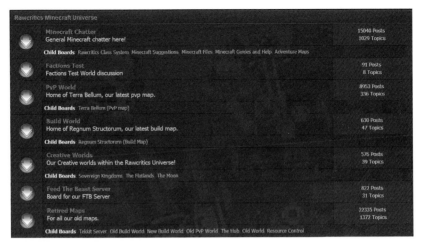

FIGURE 10.1 A Rawcritics forum page

Forums are generally good places to hang out online, but as with anything else, it's a good idea to know where your kids are spending their time. Most forums are supportive and positive, but bullying can happen. Or they could be on a forum whose tone is unsupportive or overly mature. And there is always the possibility of people trolling for an easy mark, looking for an underage person to woo or con. But common sense and open communication can counter these problems, as can paying attention to where your kids are spending their time and what they're doing. Kids need to spend time talking with people who share their interests, and it can sometimes be hard for them to find those people in their day-to-day lives, particularly if they live in a smaller town or attend a small school. Broadening your horizons to include people from other backgrounds can be an awesome experience.

Rawcritics, the forum where I spend the most time, has members ranging in age from pre-teen to 40s. Unless people give their ages, it can be hard to tell: Our teens are for the most part, incredibly mature, our older players typically don't patronize or talk down, and everyone is on equal footing, which I love. And some of our older players see it as a chance to let loose their inner child and play with abandon. Xander says he grew up as part of the Rawcritics community, and I'd have to agree. It's where he started to explore online community, and he was welcomed immediately. Our forums include players and staff from across North America, the UK, and Australia. We also have members from South America, Asia, and Europe, though not as many. There are far more males than females, but people are respectful and welcoming, and gender rarely comes into play.

On Rawcritics, many topics are concerned with Minecraft or other games, but there are an equal number on other subjects. There are threads for setting up meet-ups, sharing favorite music, and discussing television shows or movies. There are fan-based threads, like the "Daily pony thread for all things *My Little Pony*," and there are threads that talk about current memes. And there are also threads in which people reach out to the community for help, support, or advice, which is where I think we really shine.

Because there are so many players from various time zones on our forums, it is easy to find someone to chat with at any time of day or night. This is an advantage of forums: being able to find kindred spirits, get answers, or just have company whenever you want or need it. There are similar forums all across the Internet, each with its own unique feel, history, and focus. Find one where you (or your kids) feel accepted.

■ FRIENDSHIPS BASED ON COMMON GROUND

Far from being socially isolating, as is commonly thought, spending time on the Internet can be a source of solid friendships based on shared interests. I'm not suggesting that online communities are the preferred way to spend time with others, but there is much value in connecting in whatever ways make us happy, and it can be challenging to find those who share our interests. The Internet opens many doors.

Beyond in-game and forum connections, people are finding ways to communicate through programs such as Skype, Tinychat, and

Mumble, as well as social media platforms like Facebook and Twitter. Add in YouTube and livestreaming, both of which incorporate comments or chatting, and the ways to connect with our fellow human beings are constantly expanding. I find this incredibly exciting, as we are breaking down societal boundaries and inviting dialogue far beyond our own backyards.

Within our backyards, however, yet more connections around Minecraft are being formed, particularly among kids. Where I work, Minecraft is a common topic among the kids, and it gives me an instant way to connect with them as well. I love watching conversations unfold as people discover a mutual interest in the game. Wearing a Minecraft T-shirt invites dialogue and conversation, though somehow the topic comes up frequently even without a cue. I've watched friendships blossom between kids who had never connected prior, and I've seen so much creativity and mutual support as they share concerns or problems, talk about successful builds, or discuss updates and new features. Shared interests are a great way to make connections, and although some might be superficial, others may grow into deeper relationships.

MINECRAFT AND EDUCATION

One of the exciting ways that Minecraft is being used outside direct gaming is in education. As technology is appearing more and more in classrooms, it is no wonder that Minecraft, with its open-ended, creative aspects, would find its place there too.

■ HOMESCHOOLING

We've been homeschooling since Xander was in first grade. At first I was opposed to technology in learning and tried to keep the two separate. When Xander was found to be both gifted and learning-disabled in second grade, I began to explore using technology. Discovering how much of a motivator it was made incorporating it much easier. The desire to play a Pokémon video game was what finally made him successful at reading, and keeping up with chat while playing Minecraft on Rawcritics had him typing faster than me in short order.

Both e-bus and Self Design, our homeschool providers, have recognized the value of Minecraft, for which I am extremely grateful. Xander has written papers on the history of the game. He spent weeks researching Art Deco design and history and the 1927 silent film *Metropolis* so he could replicate a building in a PVP world. He was already interested in the film and likely would have written about it, but the Minecraft connection gave him further focus.

Other students have done similar projects for our homeschool programs, from setting up servers to using Minecraft to illustrate scientific principles. They submit creative projects and experiment with coding and writing simple mods. Minecraft and homeschooling complement each other well, and there are many resources and servers that are aimed at homeschooling and unschooling families.

■ MINECRAFT IN THE CLASSROOM

Teachers have recognized the potential for Minecraft in the classroom as well. It is well known that we learn more and are more motivated and engaged when the topic matches our personal interests. Tapping into this leads to success in the classroom, no matter what the motivating factor is. Minecraft is accessible and motivating in one form or another for pretty much everyone.

Countless lesson plans can be found with a simple online search. MinecraftEdu.com, a program that partners with the makers of Minecraft to provide discounts on Minecraft to schools, sells an education-specific mod pack and provides information through their forums and wiki page.

■ LITERACY

Minecraft can provide practice in both reading and writing in several ways, particularly when children are playing with others. In a single-player game, there are some opportunities for reading, such as reading labels, and books can be crafted and written within the game itself (**Figure 10.2**). Researching Minecraft can lead to reading practice as well, as players do research on wiki pages or other websites.

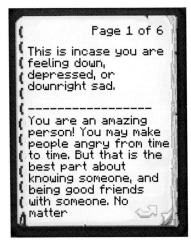

FIGURE 10.2 A page in a book by Rawcritics member Nelag

When you're playing Minecraft with others, a chat program allows players to write to each other. This is how Xander became a skilled typist. When he first started to play on Rawcritics, the chat would scroll up the screen, and once it reached the top, it disappeared. Now you can scroll it back down a few pages, in case you missed some of the chat. But when Xander first started, if he wanted to join the conversation, he had to read and respond quickly. He didn't want to be embarrassed by spelling errors, and he dislikes "text talk" (those shortcuts people use), so he asked me to post near the computer a list of words he could refer to. Xander has dysgraphia, the written-output aspect of dyslexia, so typing was a challenge for him. Because he set his own goals and got instant feedback and reinforcement in the form of chats, he was very motivated, and within a couple of months he'd vastly improved his spelling and typing.

There are also other opportunities for writing. Our server has an active lore, so a few players write the created history and post it on the forums. People write books in-game, and one of our players organizes book fairs where we can buy or trade books. The town I live in on our PVP world is a massive library. We have collected all the books written by players, and players can borrow books.

Xander has written reports on his projects. His nation on PVP, Cepheus, consists of four to six towns. He wrote a constitution for his nation and had other towns sign it. He has written his own lore. Other players write storylines for adventure maps they create, or write fiction around their Minecraft world. The opportunities for literacy are boundless.

Wrednax's Constitution

1. Every two weeks ownership of the nation will switch from one town to another to make sure no one has more control than anyone else for too long.

2. All citizens have rights decided by their current town, meaning that each town would be in charge of its own citizens.

3. Each town leader can choose one assistant of their town to be a member of the council. This would be so that if one person has to go on vacation the assistant can make decisions for them for the time they are away. It will also add to the voting pool.

4. If Cepheus ever gains a monopoly and creates a lack of combat and raiding, then it will be split in half and each side would not be allowed to ally with the other. This is so that we don't end up doing what Indoril (a rival nation) did and gaining complete power.

Wrednax

AT THE TIME OF THIS WRITING, Rawcritics is almost ready for a new PVP map, which means a fresh start for everyone. I've been designing my new town, but I'm still not sure whether to create a city below the ground, a city in the sky, or a city below the waves.

This indecision has made writing lore rather difficult, because the lore affects the town, but the town affects the lore.

For instance, if I were to build the underwater city, it would use a lot of natural blocks because the lore would say that it was a city that grew from a seed. But if I build a floating city, the lore would be that it is the ruins of an ancient city that has floated around the world for centuries with different cultures on it, so it would have a blend of styles. And I have more thoughts to choose from if I build a city on the ground, but I would use a more ragtag design, as if one city were built on the ruins of others.

My decision will be influenced in part by other players, both those who are part of my town and those fighting against it.

I like writing lore because it allows me to create a background for the game, and because it makes me feel closer to being a game designer and writer.

■ MATHEMATICS

One of the ways teachers frequently use Minecraft is in demonstrating geometry concepts. For instance, the blocks can be placed to create various forms, and they can be filled with water to demonstrate volume. But Minecraft can also be used to teach basic numeracy skills. Crafting items can help with simple problem-solving and equations, and at the very least, kids will quickly pick up on their times tables for the number eight, because objects are typically stacked in groups of eight (**Figure 10.3**).

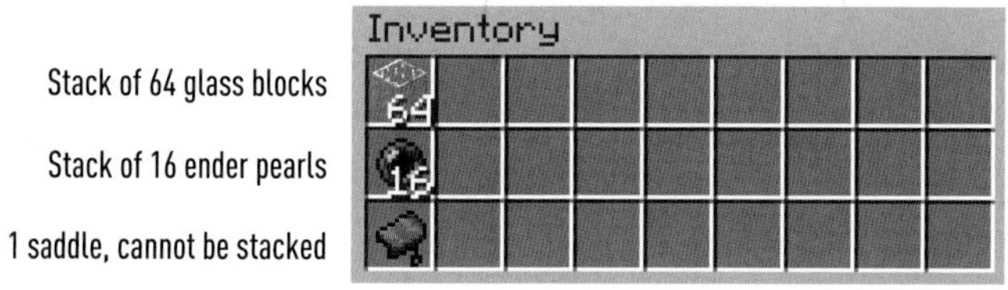

Stack of 64 glass blocks

Stack of 16 ender pearls

1 saddle, cannot be stacked

FIGURE 10.3 In Minecraft, most items are stacked in your inventory in groups of eight.

You can find many examples of teaching math concepts through Minecraft online, and the beauty of it is that it is flexible enough to be modified to suit individual needs.

■ OTHER LEARNING

From creating dioramas to building simple circuitry (see www. youtube.com/watch?v=DzSpuMDtyUU), there are as many academic applications for Minecraft as there are ideas and people willing to implement them. Teachers can use Minecraft to teach social skills, particularly those of working together toward a common goal. For example, they might set up a classroom server with a custom-designed map and assign students the task of a simple building project. Minecraft is a great tool for teaching resource management, because all resources must be mined, harvested, or traded for, meaning that players must conserve them or plan for how to acquire them.

As with any other teaching tool, these ideas will work only if they are implemented by a teacher who is prepared to put in the time and energy to create the lesson plans and materials. Not all teachers have the skills to use Minecraft in the classroom, and they shouldn't be faulted for this—everyone brings their own talent and vision to teaching. If your child's teacher does not use Minecraft, you can still find resources online and use them at home with your kids.

Although some teachers are using Minecraft in education, what kids, especially teens, are accomplishing with Minecraft outside the classroom is rarely acknowledged, and it should be. The literary, mathematical, design, and architectural aspects are amazing.

These kids should be given credit for the leadership they exhibit and the dedication they put into their work. Gamers with YouTube channels or regular livestreams, should be able to submit some of their work for credit, as should those who are in leadership roles as moderators or who work on promotions, marketing, coding, or any of the other behind-the-scenes jobs that need to be done.

I don't think this is a Minecraft-only issue. Youth are doing more and more on their own time and should be acknowledged for it.

CREATIVITY

Minecraft invites creativity far beyond the game itself, and people have used it to create across a huge variety of mediums. On the online market Etsy, you will find pages of handcrafted Minecraft-inspired items, from clothing to jewelry to curios and household objects. On YouTube you can find game tutorials, walkthroughs, and music videos. It's also possible to order Minecraft textiles and wall coverings and to find recipes for Minecraft cakes and treats.

■ CRAFTS

One way to get kids off the computer is to engage them in crafts. I'm a crafty person, and when I get fidgety I craft to keep my hands busy. I make creepers and squid with pipe cleaners (**Figure 10.4**), which your child can easily replicate.

FIGURE 10.4 Creepers made of Perler beads, pipe cleaners, and plasticine

PERLER BEADS

These are a staple at every daycare I've worked at, and I bring them with me when I'm working with kids as a nanny. Sometimes called fuse beads or melty beads, Perler beads are placed on a flat plastic pegboard and then ironed into a permanent creation. Since they are created on a grid, they lend themselves well to re-creating images from Minecraft, which are made of individual blocks.

Patterns can be found online, but if you don't have a pattern it's relatively simple to re-create any Minecraft image by using one bead for each block. Some people have gotten more creative and make 3D models of Minecraft characters by designing interlocking edges. Directions for this are also readily found online.

PAPER CONSTRUCTIONS

Folding paper or cardstock cubes is relatively simple once you have a template. Individual cubes can be glued or attached with paper brads to create a figure. There are many directions and templates available online for such activities. Using a blank template allows you to design it to look like your Minecraft character or any creation your imagination can devise. This unlimited creativity can lead to amazing designs and constructs in the hands of kids, from simple creatures to full dioramas they can use for pretend play.

DRAWING AND PAINTING

If you have kids who are already very hooked into Minecraft and are interested in drawing, chances are high that you have a Minecraft drawing or 20 already kicking around. The boxy, regular forms lend themselves well to drawing practice for budding artists, and more advanced artists sometimes put a personal spin on their creations, taking them out of the pixelated realm and portraying them in a more realistic manner.

It's easy to bring crayons and paper when you'll be waiting for an appointment or a meal at a restaurant. If your child says they don't know what to draw, suggest something from Minecraft and see what they come up with. More advanced artists can explore with other mediums and create some amazing pieces of art (**Figure 10.5**).

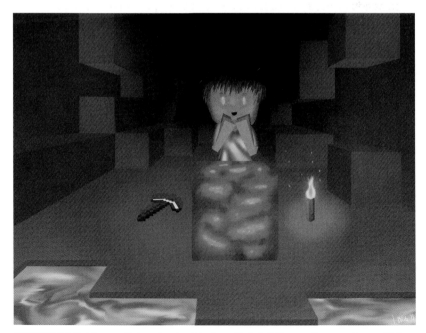

FIGURE 10.5 Minecraft-inspired art by Igor Bolek (Minecraft name AxonnPL)

MODELING CLAY

Play-Doh, plasticine, clay, and polymer clays are all fun for build-ing 3D Minecraft models. They will likely have rounded edges, which softens their appearance. It's easy to make a small cube by roll-ing the clay into a ball and then flattening the sides gently. To make rectangles for creepers or other mobs, start with a cylinder and then flatten the sides. There are other techniques for more precise cubes with sharper edges. Depending on the material, you can paint or color the finished product. A quick search online will reveal plenty of ideas and projects, from small polymer jewelry pieces to larger models.

JEWELRY

There are many ways to craft Minecraft jewelry. Beads, enamel, decoupage, shrink plastic, and polymer clays can all be used to create unique pieces. Directions for many pieces can be found with a quick search of the Internet. I find that Minecraft jewelry, even something as simple as a polymer-clay pendant, can be a fun and personal gift for the hard-to-please gamer on your list, and it is a great activity for crafty kids and teens.

DESIGNING IN CREATIVE MODE

One other way people are making amazing works of art is by using the unlimited potential of the creative map, where they don't need to worry about collecting materials or staying alive.

When it comes to building, the designs are endless and impressive. From medieval castles to spaceships and futuristic constructs, and from simple buildings to entire cities, people are designing and craft-ing. We have a creative map on Rawcritics that I love to explore just to see what people are crafting, and a quick search of YouTube will result in galleries of creative works (**Figure 10.6**).

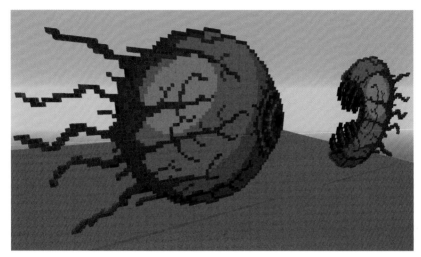

FIGURE 10.6 A detailed example of pixel art by Rawcritics player Goobachu

■ DRAMATIC PLAY

You wouldn't think at first that Minecraft would lend itself to dramatic play, but watch kids playing on the playground and you might be surprised. The kids I work with regularly act out Minecraft scenarios as they play, either taking on the roles themselves or using toys such as Lego to role-play. They are finding other ways to share their love of the game and to extend it to interactive social play.

The youth group at the community center where I work put on a series of skits last spring, and our out-of-school care group was invited to be the audience. Somehow I hadn't expected to see a Minecraft-themed skit, though in retrospect I shouldn't have been surprised, given that I'd spoken about Minecraft with many of these youth at various times. They had made costumes, written a script, and rehearsed it, and it was clearly their favorite of the skits they shared, as well as the favorite of the group of fourth and fifth graders that made up their audience. It was a fun way for the two groups to share a common interest, and the excitement of the skit carried on to the playground when the two groups ended up there together a few days later. It was another form of connection.

VIDEO

Type "Minecraft" into YouTube, and you will get thousands of results. Many of these I've covered already, such as game walkthroughs, let's plays, and tutorials. There are also creative works, reviews of mods, and my personal favorite: music videos.

One of the first ways I was exposed to Minecraft was through music videos that had been created by fans. There were just a few at the time, but they were great fun and showed the passion of the creators for this cool game. Some were song parodies, taking existing songs and turning them into new Minecraft songs, such as inthelittlewood's "Form This Way," based on Lady Gaga's "Born This Way." Some were original songs, like Tobuscus's "Diamond Sword Song." It was fun to see people's passion for the game brought to music. Since then, many more songs have been created—a recent YouTube search yielded 25 pages of results.

Some songs have basic videos that show simple images from the game, whereas others are filmed within a game with scores of players taking part. These have been edited and treated with great professionalism and skill. The range of songs, and the talent that has gone into making them, is truly impressive.

MINECON AND OTHER GATHERINGS

Players are reaching beyond the online world to extend their connections into the physical. MineCon, a convention held by Mojang, is in its third year and has gained in popularity with each one. The 2013

Minecon, with 7500 tickets available, sold out in less than five minutes, leaving tons of disappointed fans.

The Penny Arcade Expo (PAX) is a massive gaming convention that takes place in Seattle, Boston, and Australia. Minecraft and Mojang have a solid presence there—last year Xander and I were able to meet the designers who were hired when Notch stepped down, as well as attend a panel discussing upcoming changes to the game. Waiting in line for the panel allowed us to meet and talk with many players and share in their enthusiasm and excitement. Similar gatherings happen on a smaller scale at other conventions.

Local groups of players meet and play together, or simply gather without playing the game to enjoy each other's company. Sometimes these start as a group of friends or classmates; other times, players might meet in-game and then meet in person.

For a parent, it can be scary to think of your child meeting someone in person that they met online, but I try to be open to the possibilities and trust my gut. I pay attention to the people Xander plays with, and although I know people can portray themselves as something they are not, I don't feel that there is any inherent danger in being open to the possibility of a meet-up, provided there is an adult present when these meet-ups occur. When a YouTube gamer that Xander follows, PauseUnpause, posted that he would be in our city and was open to meeting up with some of his fans, I felt it was a pretty awesome opportunity. I wouldn't let Xander go on his own, and I did some checking into what the actual plans were, but we ended up joining PauseUnpause and some of his friends and fans at an arcade downtown. It was a blast. Here was someone that these kids all admired joining them on their turf, playing with them, and conversing. He signed autographs and the group went to lunch. It's a great reminder that the players on the other side of the camera are real people.

I love that Minecraft, other games, and other online communities are uniting people, giving them new ways to share their voices and their ideas with the rest of the world.

PARENT-CHILD COMPUTER CONTRACT

A COMPUTER-USE CONTRACT is a good way to make sure expectations are clear—for children and adults. This appendix includes a very basic sample contract with some suggestions for expanding it to meet your family's needs.

I cannot stress enough that the contract should go two ways. Kids need to know what the expectations are and also that their needs are being addressed.

I suggest sitting down as a family to write your contract. I also suggest starting with broad boundaries and limits and pulling them in if strong restrictions are necessary. All members of the family should agree to abide by the contract, although you may need individual contracts for different age ranges or needs.

Make sure that everyone understands all the parts of the contract, and have everyone sign it before posting it in a central location. To ensure that it is current and relevant, reassess it regularly as a family as your children become more independent.

CONTRACT

Our family understands that computer time is a privilege. We want to make using the computer fair and fun, so we agree to the following rules:

CHILDREN

1. I have _____ (minutes/hours) to use the computer. I will respect the time boundaries. I might earn bonus time and will treat that time the same way.

2. I will work to manage my time to finish a project in the time available. I will not start a project that I know will take me over my allotted time, but if a project does exceed my allotted time, I will ask you for an extension in a polite and respectful manner.

3. I will not go to websites that you have not checked to make sure they are safe and appropriate. (for younger players)

4. I will not go to restricted sites that have a minimum age.

5. I will not give out my name, address, birthday, phone number, passwords, or other personal information without checking with you.

6. I will not download anything onto the computer without checking with you, and I will patiently wait for your reply.

7. I will act in a trustworthy manner and expect that you will trust me to do so.

8. If I see or hear something that is scary or makes me uncomfortable, or if I made changes that are harming the computer, I will tell you right away, even if it is because I did something I shouldn't have.

9. I will let you know what is important to me and teach you how I use the computer so that you can understand and support me.

PARENTS

1. I will ensure that computer time is balanced and fair, and that if you need to stop early or start later due to my scheduling needs, I will allow you to "bank" that time for another session.

2. I understand that sometimes stopping a game in the middle of a project is difficult or impossible, and I will approach requests to extend gameplay with an open mind.

3. I will not snoop into your online activities without reasonable cause, and even then I will talk with you first.

4. I will extend to you the trust you wish, as long as you live up to that trust.

5. I will be open to you exploring new areas or downloading content, as long as you have asked me and given me time to research it.

6. If you come to me stating that something made you uncomfortable or scared or that you have changed something on the computer, I will take you seriously and not overreact. Nor will I become angry if you go beyond your boundaries but come to me to explain. We will deal with the situation together in a calm manner.

7. I will learn about the things you are interested in so that I can share in this part of your life and make informed decisions.

Parent:_____

Child: _____

Date: _____

ADDITIONS

Every family has different rules, guidelines, and consequences, and they will change as a child grows older and earns more trust and privileges. You might want to expand your contract to be more specific.

Here are a few issues to consider:

- Include a set, scheduled time—but only if your schedule is very consistent.

- List consequences to infractions.

- If your child needs specific guidelines, be specific about which sites are and are not allowed.

Here are some additional clauses you might include:

- I will not arrange to meet someone in person without discussing with my parents and bringing a parent along. (Use your best judgement—sometimes meetups can be safe and fun.)

- I will not purchase anything online without my parent's knowledge.

- I will not fill out forms for contests or games without my parent's knowledge.

- I will not lie about my age to gain access to sites.

- I will do my homework and chores before my computer time. (If I am finished to my parent's satisfaction ahead of schedule, I may have extra time to play.)

GLOSSARY

API (application programming interface). A programming interface that allows software to interact or fit in with other software. In Minecraft, it allows for smoother matching of the programming with mods and plugins.

blocks. The basic building material in Minecraft, blocks are approximately one meter cubes and can be anything from dirt and stone to wool or a watermelon.

caps. Using all uppercase letters when chatting online—it is considered shouting and therefore rude.

despawn. When a mob or item disappears from the game. Mobs despawn when they are killed. Player items dropped at death will also despawn after a few minutes.

enchantments. Spells that can be applied to items by using an enchanting table and experience points.

End/the End. Another dimension in the game; populated by endermen and the ender dragon.

experience points. Points that are collected during gameplay by mining, smelting, killing mobs, and breeding animals; used for enchanting items.

forums. Online discussion boards on which people can post and reply to messages.

gaming servers. Hosted websites that allow gamers to join in a multiplayer game.

griefing. Deliberately damaging or destroying other players' work; may get a player banned from many servers.

grinder/mob grinder. A setup that allows mobs to spawn and be easily trapped and killed.

grinding. A system of getting experience points by killing mobs that spawn in a grinder.

let's play (LP). A video of a gamer playing a game, usually with a commentary.

livestream. Playing a game live for an online audience, usually with a commentary.

mobs. Creatures in the game; mob stands for "mobile entity" and is a common gaming term.

mob drops. Items left, or dropped, by mobs when they are killed.

mob spawner. A dungeon cage that serves as a spawn point for mobs.

mods (modifications). Downloadable user-friendly additions or modifications to the game, usually written by other players.

Nether. The underworld of Minecraft—dark caverns filled with lava and hostile mobs.

NPCs (non-player characters). Characters that are written into the game; players can often interact with them. Villagers in Minecraft are NPCs.

Overworld. The main world in Minecraft.

plugins. Software that changes or adds to the existing program on a server.

recipe. Directions for crafting items; often take the form of a picture of the materials on a crafting bench.

redstone. A type of block that forms a powder used to make electric circuits; also the term used for the circuitry itself.

resource. The new API used by Mojang to install texture packs; now includes sound packs.

sandbox game. A game that takes place in an open world in which the player has complete freedom to explore and create and isn't restricted to an existing storyline.

screenshot/screenie. Image taken of the current screen by pressing F2; saved in the .minecraft screenshots folder.

skin. The character's appearance in the game. The default skin is "Steve." Players can download or create custom skins.

spamming. In game chat, swearing, repeating messages, insulting, posting links or web addresses, or otherwise annoying other players.

spawn. To appear in the game. Players and mobs both spawn; items can also be spawned into a game.

spawn point. The place at which a player first spawns; the spawn point can be reset by making and sleeping in a bed.

texture pack. A game modification that changes the appearance of all blocks.

walkthrough. A game tutorial, in text or video, in which a gamer plays through the game.

white-list. A system on servers where players must be approved, or placed on a "white list," in order to join.

wiki. A website that anyone can edit or add content to.

INDEX

Symbol

_ (underscore), using with usernames, 62

A

A key, action for, 96
academic applications, 218
accomplishments, documenting, 206–208
accounts
    creating separately, 58–59
    for LANs, 168
addiction
    intrinsic reward, 43
    mining, 43
Allow Cheats button, 92, 94
anvil
    crafting, 134
    using, 134
API (application programming interface), 231
arm, 77
armor
    boots, 131
    chest plate, 131
    helmet, 131
    leggings, 131
    meter, 131
    wearing, 130–131
art and text, sharing online, 199

B

baby zombie, 86–87, 114
balance, 45
base camp, creating, 141–142
bats, 110

behavior concerns, 44–45
billing information, entering, 68
biomes
    desert, 101
    End portal, 103
    examples, 99–100, 104
    explained, 99
    extreme hills, 101
    Eye of Ender, 103
    forest, 100
    Hell/Nether, 102
    jungle, 101
    mushroom island, 101–102
    Nether portal, 102–103
    plains, 100
    properties, 99
    Sky/End, 103
    swamp, 101
    taiga, 101
    traveling between, 99
birch, 123
blaze, 118
blocks
    clay, 124–125
    crafted, 126
    defined, 231
    dirt, 124–125
    explained, 2
    ores, 125–126
    organic, 126–127
    sand, 125
    sandstone, 125
    stone, 124–125
    trees, 123
    types, 122–123
    wood, 123–124
Bonus Chest button, 92, 94–95

bookshelf, 127
boots, 131
bosses
    ender dragon, 121
    withers, 120–121
boundaries, expanding, 41
brewing stand, 127
build servers, 180
building materials, 127–128
builds, 6
Buy Now button, clicking, 66
buying Minecraft
    creating Mojang account,
        63–65
    gift codes or cards, 68–69
    online, 65–68
    options for, 67–68

C

caps, defined, 231
cave spiders, 115–116
cavern, breaking through to, 142
Cepheus, 216
characters, appearance of, 149
chat program, using, 215. *See also*
    global chat; multiplayer chat;
    voice chat
chatting with children, 193–194
cheats. *See* Allow Cheats button
chest, 127
chest plate, 131
chickens, using as food, 84–85, 108
children
    chatting with, 193–194
    playing with, 193–194
    presentation of, 185–186
children's books, 26–27
classroom, Minecraft in, 214
clay, 124–125, 222
coal, 126
commands
    keyboard, 95–97
    mouse, 95–97

communication and trust, 33–36.
        See also online communication
community
    forums, 210–212
    friendships, 212–213
    livestreaming, 8
    multiplayer servers, 8
    online forums, 8
    YouTube, 7–8
computers, playing on, 25
contract
    additions, 230
    children, 228–229
    clauses, 230
    considering, 42
    parents, 229–230
conventions
    MineCon, 224–225
    PAX (Penny Arcade Expo), 225
cows, 106
crafting bench, 78–80, 127
crafting items, 127–128
crafts
    creepers, 219–220
    drawing, 221
    jewelry, 222
    modeling clay, 222
    painting, 221
    paper constructions, 220–221
    Perler beads, 220
Create New World
    menu, 76
    window, 91
Creative mode
    descending, 98
    designing in, 222–223
    flight movement, 97
    flying, 98
    inventory, 98
    movement commands, 98
    overview, 12–13
    vs. Survival mode, 13–14, 51
creativity, 219–223
creeper explosions, 54–55

creepers, 116, 219–220
crops, 137–138
crying, 48
cubes
  clay, 124–125
  crafted, 126
  defined, 231
  dirt, 124–125
  explained, 2
  ores, 125–126
  organic, 126–127
  sand, 125
  sandstone, 125
  stone, 124–125
  trees, 123
  types, 122–123
  wood, 123–124
cues, providing, 42–43
cyber-bullying, 31

D

D key, action for, 96
day, length of, 86
deaths, 87. *See also* sudden death
decorative materials, 127
desert biome, 101
despawn, defined, 231
diamond, 126, 143
difficulty settings. *See also* settings
  changing, 14–15
  Easy, 74
  Hard, 74
  managing, 75
  Normal, 74
digging, 139
dirt, 124–125
documenting accomplishments,
  206–208
dogs/wolves, 111–112
domestic animals, spawning, 105
donkeys, 108
downloading Minecraft, 70–72
dramatic play, 223–224
drawing, 221

dungeons, 93
dyslexia, 24

E

E key, action for, 96
Easy difficulty setting, 15, 74
editions
  Minecraft Pocket, 18
  Raspberry Pi, 19
  Sony PS3/PS4, 19
  Windows and Mac, 17–18
  Xbox 360, 19
education. *See also* learning
  opportunities
  classrooms, 214
  homeschooling, 213–214
  literacy, 215–216
  mathematics, 217–218
  vs. rules, 43–44
email verification, opening, 65
emerald, 126
emotional resiliency, 47–49
emotions. *See also* gaming
  emotions
  crying, 48
  and gaming, 50
  hormonal changes, 49
  managing, 45–46
enchanting
  anvil, 134
  experience points, 132–133
  objects, 133
  potions, 135
enchanting table, 127, 131–133
enchantments, defined, 231
End portal biome, 103
ender dragon, 121
endermen, 87, 111–113
End/the End, defined, 231
experience points, 132–133, 231
explosions, 54–55
extreme hills biome, 101
Eye of Ender, 103, 112

F

F1 key, action for, 96
F2 key, action for, 96
F3 key, action for, 97
F5 key, action for, 97
family routines, including games in, 55
family-friendly servers, 41
farms. *See also* food
    automated, 137–138
    crops, 137–138
    livestock, 136–137
    sizes, 136
files, accessing, 146–148
first night. *See also* night; Survival mode
    baby zombie, 86–87
    deaths, 87
    endermen, 87
    length of, 86
    spawn point, 87–88
    surviving, 74, 83, 86–87
flight movement, 97
flying, 98
food, getting, 84, 136. *See also* farming
forest biome, 100
formats
    Minecraft Pocket Edition, 18
    Raspberry Pi, 19
    Sony PS3/PS4 Edition, 19
    Windows and Mac, 17–18
    Xbox 360 Edition, 19
forums
    defined, 231
    explained, 210
    moderating, 210
    Rawcritics page, 210–212
frame for item, 127
friendly mobs. *See also* mobs
    bats, 110
    chickens, 108
    cows, 106
    donkeys, 108
    horses, 108
    mooshrooms, 107
    mules, 108–109
    ocelots/cats, 110
    pigs, 108
    sheep, 107–108
    squid, 109
    villagers, 111
friendships, 212–213
frustrations
    creeper explosions, 54–55
    getting lost, 52–53
    learning to play, 50–51
    losing items, 54
    reducing, 52–55
    sudden death, 53–54
FTB (Feed the Beast) modpack, 157–158, 161
furnace, 83, 127

G

game formats
    Minecraft Pocket Edition, 18
    Raspberry Pi, 19
    Sony PS3/PS4 Edition, 19
    Windows and Mac, 17–18
    Xbox 360 Edition, 19
game modes
    Creative, 12–13
    Hardcore, 16
    Survival, 13–15
game profile
    creating, 69–70
    username, 69
games
    including in family routines, 55
    learning opportunities, 55
    starting, 76, 90

gaming, positive aspects, 55
gaming emotions. *See also*
    emotions
    managing, 50–51
    reducing frustration, 52–55
gaming servers, 231. *See also*
    servers
getting lost, 51–53, 140, 161
ghasts, 118–119
gift cards, redeeming, 65, 68–69
gift codes, using, 65, 68–69
global chat, 187. *See also* chat
    program
gold, 126
golems
    creating, 104
    iron, 120
    snow, 119
Google account, creating, 204–205
griefing, defined, 231
grinder/mob grinder, defined, 231
grinding, defined, 232

H
Hardcore setting, 16, 74
harvesting wood, 78
health meter, 77
Hell/Nether biome, 102
helmet, 131
home servers. *See also* servers
    LAN (Local Area Network),
        165–168
    Muliplayer download, 168
    setting up, 168–172
homeschooling, 213–214
horses, 108
hostile mobs. *See also* mobs
    baby zombies, 114
    cave spiders, 115–116
    creepers, 116
    silverfish, 117

skeletons, 114–115
slimes, 116
spider jockeys, 115–116
spiders, 115–116
witches, 117
zombie villagers, 114
zombies, 114
hosting server, playing Minecraft
    from, 174–175. *See also*
    servers
house rules
    contracts, 42
    cues, 42
hunger bar, 15, 77

I
information overload, 26
ingots, 126
installing
    Minecraft, 70–72
    mods, 158–159
    skins, 149–152
    texture packs, 154–157
instant messaging, 193
inventory
    categories, 98
    illustration, 77
    navigating, 97
    opening, 78–79, 97
    stacking items in, 218
    Survival vs. Creative mode,
        98–99
    survival-style, 98
    updating, 84–85
IP address, finding, 176
ipconfig, typing, 176
iron, 126
iron golems, 120
iron tools, crafting, 14
item frame, 127

J

Java programming language, 3
jukebox, 127
jungle biome, 101
jungle wood, 123

K

keyboard commands, 95–97
kids. *See* children
killing mobs, 105

L

LAN (Local Area Network) servers, 17
LAN server, setting up, 165–168
lapis lazuli, 126
lava, being wary of, 139, 142
learning by children, 28
learning curve, 50–51
learning opportunities, 55, 218–219. *See also* education
leaves, 123
Left Shift, action for, 96
Left-click, action for, 96
leggings, 131
Lego, 26
literacy, 215–216
livestock, 136–137
livestreaming
    defined, 232
    overview, 198–199
    Twitch, 208
    Ustream, 208
    websites, 8
logged in, remaining, 90
logging in to worlds, 76
log-in page, going to, 66
logs, 123
losing items, 54
LP (let's play), 232

M

Mac game format, 17–18
Macs. *See also* OS X
    configuring servers, 172–174
    downloading and installing on, 72–73
    home servers, 170–172
magma cubes, 118–119
Manneh, Carl, 4
maps, single-player, 58–59. *See also* survival maps
Martin, George R. R., 5
mathematics, 217–218
menu page, 76
messaging, 193
Metropolis, 7, 30
MineCon convention, 224–225
Minecraft. *See also* playing Minecraft; purchasing Minecraft
    activities, 122
    Alpha version, 4
    benefits, 22
    Beta version, 4
    blocks, 2
    builds, 6
    connection, 39–40
    demo version, 3
    downloading, 70–72
    early sales, 4
    growing with, 40–41
    installing, 70–72
    mobs, 2
    opening, 90
    sales in 2013, 4
    as sandbox game, 2
    scheduling, 45
    use in classrooms, 9
    uses of, 10
    wikis, 9
Minecraft files, accessing, 146–148
Minecraft folder, 146–148

Minecraft Pocket Edition, 18
Minecraft Store, 67
MinecraftEdu.com, 214
Minecraft.net, getting to, 66
mineshafts, 93
mining
    as addiction, 43
    avoiding trouble, 142–143
    base camp, 141–142
    branch-mining, 140
    locations, 139–140
    methods, 140
    preparing for, 139
mob drops, 105, 232
mob spawner, defined, 232
mobs. *See also* friendly mobs;
    hostile mobs; nether mobs;
    neutral mobs; player-created
    mobs
    appearance, 104
    breeding, 106
    defined, 232
    domestic animals, 104
    explained, 2
    killing, 105
    NPC (non-player character),
        104
    spawning, 104
    taming, 106
    types, 104
    villagers, 104
mods
    defined, 232
    explained, 3, 157–158
    installing, 158–159
    OptiFine, 159
    Rei's Minimap, 159–160
    selecting, 159
    sharing online, 202
    source, 158
Mojang account, creating, 63–65
monsters
    baby zombies, 114
    cave spiders, 115–116

creepers, 116
silverfish, 117
skeletons, 114–115
slimes, 116
spider jockeys, 115–116
spiders, 115–116
witches, 117
zombie villagers, 114
zombies, 114
mooshrooms, 102, 107
mouse commands, 95–97
movies, 24, 201–202
mules, 108–109
multiplayer chat. *See also* chat
    program
    etiquette, 187–188
    greeting, 188
    joining, 187
    spamming, 188
    use of caps, 188
multiplayer Minecraft, 16–17
multiplayer servers, 8
mushroom island biome, 101–102
music disc, 127
music videos, sharing online,
    201–202
My Little Pony, 8, 16

N

Nelag, 215
The Nether, 12
Nether, defined, 232
nether mobs. *See also* mobs
    blaze, 118
    ghasts, 118–119
    magma cubes, 118–119
    wither skeletons, 118
Nether portal biome, 102–103
neutral mobs. *See also* mobs
    endermen, 112–113
    wolves/dogs, 111–112
    zombie pigmen, 113

night, length of, 86. *See also* first night
Normal difficulty setting, 15, 74
Notch, 4
Novaskin, 149–150
NPC (non-player character), 232
nuggets, 126

O

oak, 123
objects, enchanting, 133
ocelots/cats, 110
online communication, 186–188. *See also* communication and trust
online forums, 8
online safety
    communication and trust, 33–36
    establishing trust, 36–37
    overview, 32, 184–186
    paying attention, 38
    privacy, 37–38
online sharing. *See also* safety online
    art and text, 199
    livestreaming, 198–199
    mods, 202
    movies, 201–202
    music videos, 201–202
    options for, 196–197
    reason for, 196
    safety, 203
    skins, 202
    texture packs, 202
    tutorials, 200
    vlogs, 201
    walkthroughs, 200–201
    YouTube, 197–198
online technology, 29–32
online time
    monitoring, 43
    planning, 43
opening

inventory, 97
Minecraft, 90
OptiFine, 159–160
ores
    mined, 126
    mining for, 82
    raw, 126
    using, 125–126
organic blocks, 126–127
OS X. *See also* Macs
    accessing Minecraft files, 146–147
    downloading Minecraft, 72–73
Overworld, defined, 232

P

painting, 221
paper constructions, 220–221
passwords
    creating, 62
    entering, 64
PAX (Penny Arcade Expo), 225
Peaceful mode, 15, 54
Perler beads, 220
Persson, Markus, 3
pick axe
    making, 81–82
    using with ores, 126
picture, 127
pigs, 108
plains biome, 100
planks, 123
play is children's work, 28–29
player-created mobs. *See also* mobs
    iron golems, 120
    snow golems, 119
players
    ability to create, 6
    options for, 5
    protecting, 104
    on servers, 179–180
    types, 6

playing Minecraft. *See also*
   Minecraft
   with children, 193–194
   from hosting server, 174–175
   outside network, 176
   on servers, 178
   on Windows home network,
      175–176
plugins
   defined, 232
   using with servers, 164
Porser, Jakob, 4
potions, 135
Potter, Harry, 26–27
privacy online, 37–38
profile
   creating, 69–70
   username, 69
protecting players, 104
public servers, 177–178. *See also*
   servers
purchasing Minecraft. *See also*
   Minecraft
   creating Mojang account,
      63–65
   gift codes or cards, 68–69
   online, 65–68
   options for, 67–68
PVP (player-versus-player) world,
   30

Q

Q key, action for, 96
quartz, 126

R

Raspberry Pi, 19
Rawcritics multiplayer server, 8–9
recipes, 232
redstone circuitry, 126, 143, 232
Rei's Minimap, 159–160
resource, defined, 232
resource packs, 153, 156

respawning, 14
Right-click, action for, 96
roleplaying, 180
routers, 176
rules vs. education, 43–44

S

S key, action for, 96
safety online. *See also* sharing
   online
   communication and trust,
      33–36
   establishing trust, 36–37
   overview, 32, 184–186
   paying attention, 38
   privacy, 37–38
sand, 87, 125
sandbox game, 2, 232
sandstone, 125
saplings, 123
screen, clearing, 206
screen time, degrees of, 24–27
screenshots, taking, 206
screenshot/screenie, 233
server hosts, 177
server setup, troubleshooting, 177
servers. *See also* gaming servers;
   home servers; hosting server;
   public servers
   accessing, 164–165
   adding, 181–182
   anti-griefing, 183
   behavior, 183
   build type, 180
   and community, 179–180
   configuring, 172–174
   explained, 164, 231
   family-friendly, 41
   finding, 180–181
   finding IP address, 176
   guidelines, 182–184
   joining, 181–182
   LAN (Local Area Network), 17

servers (*continued*)
    language, 183
    mod restrictions, 183–184
    multiplayer, 8
    playing on, 16, 164, 178
    plugins, 164
    Rawcritics, 8–9
    saving, 181–182
    sharing, 176
    staffing, 182–183
    stopping from running, 172
    themed type, 180
    types, 180
    WesterosCraft, 5–6
settings, choosing, 41. *See also*
    difficulty settings
sharing online. *See also* safety
    online
    art and text, 199
    livestreaming, 198–199
    mods, 202
    movies, 201–202
    music videos, 201–202
    options for, 196–197
    reason for, 196
    safety, 203
    skins, 202
    texture packs, 202
    tutorials, 200
    vlogs, 201
    walkthroughs, 200–201
    YouTube, 197–198
sharing servers, 176
sheep, 107–108
shelters, making, 82, 84–85
sign, 127
silverfish, 117.
skeletons, 114–115. *See also* wither
    skeletons
Skindex, 149–150
skins
    browsing, 151
    changing, 151
    creating, 152

    defined, 233
    editing, 152
    explained, 149
    finding, 149
    installing, 149–152
    locating, 151
    sharing online, 202
Sky/End biome, 103
Skype, 190–193
slabs, 123
slimes, 116
snow golems, 119
A Song of Ice and Fire, 5
Sony PS3/PS4 Edition, 19
Spacebar, action for, 96
spamming, 233
spawn, defined, 233
spawn point
    appearing at, 76
    defined, 233
    distance from, 87–88
    explained, 77
spawning domestic animals, 105
spider jockeys, 115–116
spiders, 115–116
spruce, 123
squid, 109
stairs, 123
Star Trek, 16
start menu, 75
starting
    games, 90
    worlds, 91
sticks, crafting for pick, 81–82
stone, 124–125
stone tools, making, 82–83
Store page, going back to, 67
strongholds, 93
structures
    dungeons, 93
    generating, 93
    mineshafts, 93
    strongholds, 93
    villages, 93

sudden death, 53–54. *See also* deaths
Survival game, starting, 75–77
survival maps. *See also* maps
    remaining on, 54
    starting games on, 74
Survival mode. *See also* first night
    vs. Creative mode, 13–14, 51
    difficulty levels, 14–15
    dying in, 14
    Easy difficulty setting, 15
    game settings, 74–75
    Hard difficulty setting, 15
    iron tools, 14
    Normal difficulty setting, 15
    Peaceful difficulty setting, 15
    playing on, 74
    respawning, 14
swamp biome, 101
sword, making from stone, 82–83

T

T key, action for, 96
Tab key, action for, 97
table, enchanting, 127
taiga biome, 101
technology
    changing role of, 23
    cyber-bullying, 31
    degrees of screen time, 24–27
    online, 29–32
    play as children's work, 28–29
    positive aspects, 55
television, 24
terrain. *See* biomes
text and art, sharing online, 199
texture packs
    defined, 233
    downloading, 155
    explained, 152–153
    installing, 154–157

sharing online, 202
themed servers, 180
time, measuring, 86
tools
    constructing, 128
    crafting bench, 78–80
    enchanting, 125–126
    harvesting wood, 78
    levels of efficiency, 129
    making out of stone, 82–83
    making shelters, 82
    mining for ores, 82
    naming, 128–129
    pick axe, 81–82
    recipes, 129
    repairing, 128–129
    torches, 85
    wearing down, 128
torches
    making, 85
    using as markers, 53
Tower of Babel, 7, 29–32
trees
    birch, 123
    chopping down, 124
    jungle wood, 123
    leaves, 123
    logs, 123
    oak, 123
    planks, 123
    saplings, 123
    slabs, 123
    spruce, 123
    stairs, 123
trouble, avoiding, 142–143
trust
    in Cori's house, 33–36
    establishing, 36–37
    learning about, 40
tutorials, sharing online, 200–201
Twitch, 208

U

underscore (_), using with
usernames, 62
usernames
  choosing long term, 62
  creativity, 61–62
  entering for profiles, 69
  length, 61
  privacy, 60
  selecting, 59–60
  simplicity, 61
  using underscore (_), 62
Ustream, 208

V

video. *See also* YouTube
  capturing, 207
  uploading, 207–208
  YouTube, 224
video games
  emotions associated with, 50
  views on, 22, 25
villagers, 104, 111
villages, 93
vlogs, sharing online, 201
voice chat. *See also* chat program
  call safety, 190
  equipment, 189–190
  overview, 188–189
  Skype account, 190–192
  types of, 189

W

W key, action for, 96
walkthroughs
  defined, 233
  sharing online, 200–201
waypoints, 161
weapons, 130
WesterosCraft collaborative server,
  5–6

white-list, defined, 233
wiki, 9, 233
wiki site, bookmarking, 90
Windows
  accessing Minecraft files,
    146–147
  configuring servers, 172–174
  downloading and installing on,
    71–72
  game format, 17–18
  home network, 175–176
  home servers, 169–170
  Macs, 170–172
witches, 117
wither skeletons, 118. *See also*
  skeletons
withers, 120–121
wolves/dogs, 111–112
wood
  birch, 123
  harvesting, 78
  jungle, 123
  oak, 123
  spruce, 123
World Options window, 92
world *seeds*, 92–93
World Type button
  Default setting, 94
  described, 93
  Large Biome setting, 94
  Superflat setting, 94
worlds
  arm, 77
  creating, 75–77
  Creative mode, 97–99
  health meter, 77
  hunger bar, 77
  inventory, 77
  logging into, 76
  options for, 91
  starting, 91

Wrednax
    Constitution, 216
    dyslexia, 24
    FTB (Feed the Beast) modpack,
        161
    learning about trust, 40
    oligarchical nation, 30
    playing on servers, 178
    Rawcritics PVP map, 217
    texture packs, 154
    Tower of Babel, 7, 29–32
writing, opportunities for, 216

X

Xander. *See* Wrednax
Xbox 360 Edition, 19

Y

YouTube, 7–8, 197–198, 204–206.
    See also video

Z

zombie, baby, 86–87
zombie pigmen, 113
zombie villagers, 114
zombies, 104, 114